Secrets of the Gy

SECRETS OF THE GYPSIES

KAY HENWOOD

Illustrations by John Walsh
Diagrams by Tony Barrs

A Piccolo Original

PAN BOOKS LTD
LONDON

First published 1974 by Pan Books Ltd,
33 Tothill Street, London SW1

ISBN 0 330 23942 2

Printed in Great Britain by
Richard Clay (The Chaucer Press), Ltd, Bungay, Suffolk

CONTENTS

LIST OF ILLUSTRATIONS

(*Between pages 64 and 65*)

ONE

Who are the Romanies?

Gypsies make an impression on everyone. Whether you think of them as picturesque and romantic, or just slovenly rogues, one thing is quite certain – they are one of the most fascinating groups of people in the world today. In the midst of our materialistic fast-moving twentieth century, they are amazingly loyal to their old traditions and ways of life, following occupations and customs originating over a thousand years ago.

Although, even today, many cannot read or write, the Romanies, as pure-bred Gypsies are called, pass on their manners and customs, folklore and secrets, by word of mouth, from generation to generation.

A thousand years ago these nomads began making their way from their native India, working as best they could, adjusting themselves to whatever environment they found themselves in, and largely living off the land. Gradually, during the fourteenth, fifteenth and sixteenth centuries they spread through most parts of Europe, arriving in Britain in about the year 1500. But whether wandering from one country to another, or just within the one country, one thing is necessary to the Romany: he *must* travel. It is in his bones.

He has inherited this wanderlust and it is as vital to him as the very air he breathes.

No one quite knows why these Indian people began their migration. Doubtless they were wanderers within their own original territory, but the reason why they left India was probably persecution, either by their fellow-countrymen, or foreign invaders. Of a very low caste (social order), their occupations were those considered beneath the dignity of all higher castes. They included those of mountebanks (sellers of quack medicines), fortune-tellers, players of games of chance, palmists, professional astrologers, animal-trainers, dancers, singers and musicians, horse-traders and smiths. A strange collection of occupations to be considered distasteful to upper castes, but it is curious to find that today Gypsies still follow the very occupations of their forebears in the first century BC.

As the Gypsies travelled across Europe, historians have found that they adapted themselves to their surroundings remarkably well, taking advantage of the differing circumstances in each country to make a living – but always within the framework of their own habits. A good example of this adaptability is the Gypsy who now deals in cars as he formerly dealt in horses, and the scrap merchant, who at one time would have been a skilful metal-smith. So it was that those early migrators exchanged bullocks pulling heavy wooden carts, for donkeys or handcarts, for the old-style Gypsy caravan, up to the present-day motor-trailer.

Although the horse has for long been the friend and servant of the better-off Romanies, the caravan has only been in use in fairly recent times. The so-called 'traditional' gaily painted and carved caravan has been in use for a comparatively short period – only from the end of the last century. Before that, there were rough canvas-covered, horse-drawn wagons, or hand-carts in which to carry around the tents that were their homes, and their few modest possessions and tools of trade. Even today, particularly in Spain, there are

Gypsies who carry all they possess around on their backs, or a donkey will carry a woman and a couple of small children, with panniers filled with belongings and perhaps another child, whilst the man of the family and older children walk alongside. In Britain, although there are still a few horse-drawn caravans and wagons, most Romanies will be found in modern motorized caravans. You can see them parked by the roadside, on heath and common land, or in the field of a farmer, who will employ them for the temporary work on a farm such as fruit and vegetable picking.

Inevitably, by these caravans will be the smouldering fire, or *yog* as it is called in the old Romany language. This is always the centre-piece of the Gypsy camp. Even though most caravans these days have up-to-date cooking facilities, they are rarely used. Romanies prefer, except in the very worst weather, to cook on an open fire. In the evenings they will all squat down around the fire, or sit on an upturned bucket or other handy object, to talk and maybe sing. And on special occasions this *yog* becomes the centre of very festive activities, for no one can celebrate as whole-heartedly as a Romany when he has a mind to. Feasting and drinking, story-telling, music, song and dance can occasionally continue for days on end – and always around this glowing fire, whose warmth attracts the Gypsies like a magnet.

The Romanies love and spoil their children. Although they are brought up in Spartan conditions and must learn early independence, their childhood is often idyllically happy. There is a Romany called Silvester Gordon Boswell who claims, quite sincerely, to have played with the fairies, together with his brother and sisters, when he was a boy. He says he knows people will think him 'light in the head' when he makes this claim, but he reckons that it was the supreme happiness of his childhood which put him in contact with these spirits of nature.

Romany children have few, if any, toys – but the wealth

and freedom of the countryside is forever on their doorsteps!
They learn early the names of birds, trees and plants, the
habits of wild animals, and the secrets of the elements. Such
toys as they have are not bought from shops, but fashioned
from wood with a knife, or perhaps a doll is made with rags, a
cardboard box will serve as a wagon, and a branch of a tree
will become a hobby-horse.

Being so fond of children, both for their own sake and for
the sake of continuing their heritage, Romany families tend
to be large. Usually the parents and small children sleep in
the caravan, whilst the older boys sleep in a tent. Since
families tend to travel in groups, the children have plenty of
companionship, and you will usually see a horde of scruffy
but happy-looking children around any Gypsy encampment.

In Britain each Gypsy family will have its regular route,
perhaps covering two or three counties. Romany families like
to travel in groups, but the days of large groups of twenty to
thirty wagons all travelling the road together are past,
because of the present scarcity of stopping places, and
growing number of regulations about the use of land. With
our population increasing so rapidly, land becomes more and
more scarce and precious, and it is perhaps understandable
that landowners and local authorities resent the Gypsies' free
use of it. Every acre these days must be fully and profitably
used, and it becomes more and more difficult for Gypsies to
find a stopping place. Added to this, of course, is the average
man's suspicion of Gypsies. Although regarded as mysterious
and attractive, they have, paradoxically enough, always been
held in fear and suspicion by us non-gypsies, or *gorgios* as we
are called in Romany. This is not entirely unjustified: the
landowner will usually have the job of clearing away the litter
left by the Gypsies, and, of course, the Romany will not be
troubled by his conscience when it comes to poaching the
evening meal for his family! However, you will not find a true
Romany stealing on any grand scale as is often supposed. He

will take what he requires for immediate use because he believes that the fruits and creatures of God's earth are for the benefit of mankind in general, not specifically for the owner as in the eyes of *our* law!

Of course many who travel our roads are not Romanies, and other travellers living the Gypsy life do not necessarily abide by their law. Many of these lawless folk have given 'Gypsies' in general, a bad name. In Britain today, there are about 50,000 people known as 'Gypsies', but in fact only about 10,000 of these are true Romanies. Half-blood Romanies are called *Posh-rats* (literally Romany for half-bloods) and there are about 10,000 of them. Those of mixed blood, less than half of which is Romany, are called *Didakais*; there are about 10,000 of them. The remaining 10,000 are known simply as travellers and have no connection whatever with the *Rom*, as the Romanies call themselves. They include all types of people who, for various (and not always good) reasons, want to lead a roving life.

The Romanies regard all other nomads as their inferiors, and travellers in their turn will not generally associate themselves with the *Rom*.

Romanies don't like to marry outside their own race, but in this country, with its relatively small Romany population which has been roaming our island for many generations, it has become fairly acceptable to marry a *gorgio*. On the Continent, this could mean banishment from the tribe – the very worst punishment possible!

British Romanies are a lot more integrated with their adopted land than their counterparts in Europe, but you can be sure that the Romanies will only assimilate the ways and customs that suit them. Although very adaptable when necessary, you will only find them adopting a way of life when it pleases them. So, if an English Romany seems more English than a French Romany seems French, you may be quite certain that it suits him to be so! And although the

Romanies of this country have adopted a few of our customs, they still live very differently from the *gorgios*.

Except for about three or four months of the year, the Romanies are on the road, never spending more than a few days at each stopping place. During the winter months, most

of them will stay in one place until the very first hint of spring, when their restless natures will not be satisfied unless they resume their travels. St Valentine's Day, 14 February, is the traditional date to get the caravan moving.

Romany men are the world's horse experts. Nowadays, of course, there is comparatively little horse-trading carried out, but even so a Gypsy will keep a horse or two if at all possible. Their affinity with horses is quite extraordinary. In many countries they are considered more skilled and knowledgeable than veterinary surgeons when it comes to illness, and there isn't a trick they don't know about horse-faking! Naturally, with these qualities they make excellent horse-dealers. A Gypsy can buy a poor broken-down old horse, and in the space of a fortnight transform him into quite a spirited, young-looking animal! More details of how in a later chapter.

Other favourite Romany occupations are those of smith and metal-worker, circus entertainer, animal-trainer and exhibitor, basket-maker, knife-grinder; and, in season, they take work on farms, picking fruit. A Romany will take on most kinds of work, but on two conditions: that it is an open-air job, and a temporary one. You hardly ever see Gypsies working indoors, and they take care not to shackle themselves with permanent jobs.

As well as being good wives and mothers the women go out hawking. They take their hawking baskets filled with various items that they or the men have made: clothes pegs, wooden toys, paper or woodshaving flowers, lace, or little baskets which they fill with primroses or other flowers. Sometimes they will sell wild watercress or heather, or flowers which they have picked, and these will be mixed with cheap articles, bought perhaps from Woolworths, to attract the eye of the housewives they call upon. Many of them read a palm for the traditional piece of silver, and do seem to possess an extra-ordinary power of insight. They are also uncanny experts at telling the cards, crystal-gazing, providing spells, amulets and talismans, and are perhaps most skilled of all as herbalists.

Of course all these occupations can be followed as they travel around, and contrary to popular belief, Gypsies are hard-working people. Holidays are unheard of; to take a break would mean no money. If a Romany man finds it difficult to get work during his stationary winter period, then he must live on the money he has put by during the previous summer months. Although his life is one of extreme simplicity (he scorns most material possessions), the Romany is sometimes quite wealthy.

A lot of their food is gleaned from field and wood, and some is bartered for by the women in exchange for something from the hawking basket, so the two meals a day that a Gypsy family habitually eat, are provided quite economically. A simple breakfast and a hearty meal in the evening is all that they need. Over-eating, they believe, dulls the wits, and slows down the body. One of the *gorgios'* troubles, they feel!

The word *gorgio* means clodhopper or bumpkin in Romany, and that is how they sum us up! They will never take a *gorgio* into their confidence, and to get a straight and honest answer from a Romany is almost impossible. They give the impression of trying hard to be helpful, but of nevertheless being quite stupid. This is just a ruse so that they can be as vague and evasive as they like. If a *gorgio* should believe all a Romany tells him, he is considered the greatest fool!

Gypsies are extremely loyal and faithful to each other and never give away information about themselves or their brothers. There have been fast friendships between Romany and *gorgio*, but on the whole the *gorgio* is the Romany's main enemy. It is the *gorgio* who enforces all the laws and restrictions, which to the Romany seem unnatural and unnecessary. The Romany, who can see no reason why he shouldn't camp where he likes, or kill a rabbit in a nearby field, is equally scornful of the laws which forbid him to marry under a certain age, settle an argument with his fists, require him to register births, deaths and marriages, or, in fact, any aspect of our neat and tidy bureaucratic society. It is not, however, that the Romanies are a lawless bunch: on the contrary, they are very disciplined *within their own system of law*, it's just that their laws are different from ours!

The Romany usually looks different from other roadside travellers. He may not have the classic black hair, hook-nose and high cheekbones, but he will nearly always be dark skinned, with eyes that are dark, deep-set, alert and shining.

A baby girl has her ears pierced very early in life, for all women and girls like to wear gold earrings. Gypsies are fond of bright jewellery and the women usually have quite a selection, which may be quite valuable, as they have a liking for gold which is well set off by their dark complexions. Their entire collection may be worn together on special occasions. The women always wear an apron, or *joddakai*, just as the men are usually to be seen with a *dicklo*, or neckerchief, around their necks.

The ancient Romany language is based on Sanskrit, the language of their forbears in India. Of course, it has absorbed many words from the different countries in which the Romanies have travelled, including Britain, but it remains, nevertheless, a very strange tongue to our ears. This, naturally, is to the Gypsies' advantage: it helps to preserve many of their secrets, and in front of the law can often get them out of trouble. A couple of words to a child can send it off to obtain a current driving licence from a relative, for example.

A few *gorgios* have been able to study this secret tongue, and here is a small selection from the vocabulary:

Aava – Yes
Adoi – There
Adoosta – Plenty, enough
Adoova – That
Adrail – Through
Adre – In, into, to
Adrom – Away
Agal – Before
Akei – Here
Akonyo – Alone
Amandi – To me
Amendi or *mendi* – We
And – To bring

Apre – Upon, on, or up
Atch – To stop
Atch apre – Awake, get up
Av – To come
Bang – Devil
Barvalo – Wealthy
Bauri – Snail
Bauro – Big
Baval – Wind
Beeno – Born
Besh – To sit, or year
Bik – To sell
Bishno – Rain

Bok – Hunger, or luck, fortune
Booti – Work
Bosh – To fiddle
Chal – Fellow, chap
Chavies – Children
Chei – Daughter, girl
Cheriklo – Bird
Chik – Dirt, mud, ashes, sand, soil, etc
Chin – To cut, dig
Chiv – To put
Choom – Moon
Choori – Knife
Chooro – Poor, humble
Choovikon – Witch
Cosh – Stick
Dadus – Father
Dash – Cup
De – The
Dei – Mother
Dik – To see, look
Dinilo – Fool
Divvus – Day
Dood – Light
Door – Far, or long
Doosh – Evil, bad, unlucky
Doosta – Enough, plenty, or very
Doovel – God
Drom – Road
Dukker – To tell fortunes
Fiz – Enchantment, charm

Gavengro – Policeman
Ghiv – To sing
Grei – Horse
Hol – To eat
Holomus – Feast, supper
Hono – Angry, cross
Hookapen – A lie
Horri – Penny
Hotch – To burn
Hotchi-witchi – Hedgehog
Jal – To go
Jin – To know
Jiv – To live
Jookel – Dog
Joovel – Woman
Kair – House, or to do, make, etc
Kam – Sun
Kanna – When, or now
Kek – No, not
Kekavi – Kettle
Kepsi – Basket
Kin – To buy
Kitchema – Public House
Kokero – Self, lonely, alone
Kom – To love, owe, or want
Koor – To fight, strike, knock
Kooshko-bok – Happiness, good health, good luck
Kooshto – Good
Koppa – Blanket
Kor – To call
Latch – To find

Lav – Word, name
Lel – To take, get
Lendi – To them, them, or their
Libena – Beer
Loor – To rob, steal
Mandi – I, or me
Maur – To kill
Mauro – Bread
Meero – My
Mel – To die
Men – We, us
Mol – Wine
Mong – To beg or request
Moosh – Man
Mumbli – Candle
Muterimongeri – Tea
Nafalo – Ill
Nash – To run
O – The
Paani – Water
Pal – Brother, mate
Pand opre! – Shut up!
Patser – To believe
Peer – To walk
Peeri – Cauldron, stewpan
Pek – To roast
Pen – To say, tell, or sister
Petal – Horseshoe
Piaben – Drink
Pobengro – Cider
Pobo – Apple
Pog – To break
Poorav – To bury

Pooro – Old
Pootch – To ask
Poov – Earth, or field
Pordo – Full, heavy
Posh – Half
Posha – Near, by, or besides
Praster – To run
Raati – Night
Rak – To guard, take care of
Rakli – Girl
Raklo – Boy
Rat – Blood
Rauni – Lady
Rei – Gentleman
Rikeno – Pretty
Rod – To search
Roker – To talk
Rom – Husband, bridegroom, male Gypsy
Romer – To marry
Romni – Wife, bride, female Gypsy
Rook – Tree
Roop – Silver
Roozlo – Strong
Rov – To cry
Rozali – Flower
Sal – To laugh
Sap – Snake
Sar – With
Sar shan? – How are you?
Shiv – Snow

Shookar – Nicely, quietly, slowly
Shooko – Dry
Shool – To whistle
Shoon – To hear, listen
Shushi – Rabbit
Simensa – Cousin, relation
Simmer – To pawn, pledge
Siv – To sew
Sken – Sun
Soom – To smell
Sooti – To sleep
Sor – Everything, all
Soski – Why, for what
Soverhol – To swear
Steripen – Prison
Ta – And
Tan – Camp, place, tent
Tarder – To pull, stretch
Tarno – Young
Tatcho – Good, true, right, real, holy, ready, healthy, well, safe
Tatter – To warm
Tikno – Small
Til – To hold
Too – You

Tood – Milk
Toof – Smoke
Toogno – Sorry
Torro – High
Tov – To wash
Trash – To fear, frighten, astonish
Troosh – Thirst
Troostal – About, of concerning
Tullo – Fat
Vardo – Cart, wagon, caravan
Varo – Flour
Varter – To watch
Veena – Excuse
Vel – To come
Vesh – Forest, wood
Vongar – Money, or coal
Vonka – When
Wafedo – Bad
Walgaurus – Fair
Wen – Winter
Woodrus – Bed
Woosher – To throw
Yooso – Clean, clear

Many people would be surprised to learn that several English words and slang expressions are derived from Romany. We frequently hear the word *pal*, which is the Romany for brother, and *cosh*, which is Romany for stick. We say, 'chop and change'. *Chop* is the Romany word for exchange or swap. *Tatting* is the word for rag-collecting and a *tatter* is someone who collects rags and scraps. Surely this is the origin of our slang word, tatty? *Shindy, chivvy, bosh, gibberish, tiny, toff, duffer,* and *mug* meaning face, are all claimed by language experts to be derived from Romany. Even Shakespeare, in naming the monster in 'The Tempest', chose *Caliban,* Romany for black!

Here in translation are some Romany proverbs and sayings:

'When the wind is high, move the tent to the other side of the hedge.' (Change sides in an emergency.)

'Always go by the day.' (Act according to the situation.)

'Cut your coat according to your fancy.' (Gypsy variation of the old proverb.)

'Nice reeds make nice baskets.'

'I wash my own shirt.' (Indicating unmarried independence.)

'It is always the largest fish that falls back into the water.'

'The devil in your heart. The devil in your body.' (This is an insult commonly used by Gypsies all over the world.)

'Keep a secret in your own heart and nobody will know it.'

'It's like a kiss, good for nothing until it is divided between two.'

'A cloudy morning often changes to a fine day.' (A bad start often has a good finish.)

'No man ever got money enough.'

'Behind bad luck comes good luck.'

'All men have not the same tastes.'

'Well begun is half done.'

'While you are talking the hours fly.'

'The best is soonest gone.'

'To see an old friend is as agreeable as a good meal.'

'When your brothers quarrel don't you meddle.'

'When a man gives you a horse you must not look in his mouth.' (Don't look for faults in a gift.)

'There is a sweet sleep at the end of a long road.'

'Make the best of it.'

'The bee makes the honey.' (Each does his own work.)

'The bee gets honey from flowers.' (Seeks it in the right place.)

'Wait till the moon rises.' (A very common Gypsy saying.)

'One man can take a horse to water, but twenty can't make him drink.'

'He's hungry enough to eat his shoes.'

'You can do a thing better if you go about it secretly.'

'He killed both of us.' (A sarcastic expression.)

'A bird in the hand is worth two in the hedge.'

TWO

Births, Deaths and Marriages

From birth to death the Romany follows a way of life totally different from ours.

The Gypsies' love of children is such that if for one reason or another they don't have any, it is the greatest misfortune that can befall them. Motherhood marks the fulfilment of a Romany woman's life. While she is waiting for her baby to be born she will surround herself with beautiful objects in the belief that they will make the child beautiful. She may also wear a charm of crayfish shells and stag beetles to ward away the pains of childbirth. Of course, these days many Gypsy women do not really *believe* in the efficiency of these charms, but as with many of our own customs the superstition lingers.

In some places a Gypsy woman who is expecting a child will place one of her garments under a willow tree on the eve of St George's Day. If in the morning she finds a fallen leaf on the garment she knows that the confinement will be easy.

A Romany is traditionally born on straw, always outside the caravan, and usually in a tent. When the time for the birth is near the family will find a quiet place to camp, where they can be sure of being able to remain undisturbed for a while. The midwife is usually just an older woman of the tribe with no formal medical knowledge, only experience, and a fund of Romany superstition.

When labour begins, the bed of straw is made up, perhaps in a tent, or even under the wagon, if it is the horse-drawn type which is quite high off the ground and can be screened with sacking. The children like this job of gathering straw for 'the nest'. From the very beginning of their lives they learn to accept birth and death for the perfectly natural phenomena that they are. These subjects are not taboo in the Gypsy camp: children are brought up to face life fully, both in sorrow and in joy. The whole procedure of childbirth is carried out with the minimum of fuss and disturbance, and the mother will very soon be back to living her normal life, taking the new-born baby with her when hawking.

A new-born baby will have two baptisms. One is the conventional baptism of whichever religion is officially practised by the family. If the birth is registered (it isn't always), the infant will be given a name for use by the *gorgio*, and this is the name the child will use throughout his life for all official purposes. The other ceremony, however, is more important to the Romany. It consists of immersion (if possible in running water) in the presence of the child's Godfather (*kirvo*) and Godmother (*kirvi*). The child is then given a secret name, to be used only among the Gypsies themselves.

There is yet a third name given to a Romany, and that is the most secret of all: it is whispered by the mother when the child is first born, and never mentioned again afterwards. This is designed to deceive demons, who, it is believed, can only have power over the child if they know its true identity.

Continental Gypsies of the Kalderash tribe have romantic-sounding names such as these:

Boys	Girls
Balo, Barfko, Bidshika, But-	Boti, Dunicha, Keja, Lala,
sulo, Chavula, Fero, Frin-	Lyuba, Mala, Malilini,

kelo, Hanzi, Ilika, Kalia, Oraga, Orka, Pesha, Rupa,
Kore, Luluvo, Milosh, Miya, Savina, Saviya, Tekla,
Nanosh, Pulika, Putzina, Tereina, Tshaya.
Terkari, Vaya, Yakali, Yer-
ko, Yojo.

The English Romany names can be romantic-sounding
too but, on the whole, British Romanies choose the usual
English Christian names with a preference for ones from the
Old Testament. Sometimes, however, the Romany parent
takes a fancy to the name of a poet, battle, place, etc. Here
are a few of the more fanciful and curious:

Boys	*Girls*
Adolphus, Albi, Amossy, Bendigo, Benji, Bohemius, Byron, Chiriklo, Dover, Dui, Finney, Hapsy, Ithal, Kenza, Lally, Loverin, Lumas, Manfo, Moses, Nelson, Nezer, Noah, Pyramus, Shadrack, Trafalgar, Westarus.	Athaliah, Cinderella, Coralina, Evergreen, Gerandi, Homi, Hona, Lavanya, Lavendi, Leda, Menia, Menti, Nation, Richenda, Richi, Ryalla, Shuri, Sinfi, Reubina, Vashni, Zena.

There is a Gypsy of the well-known Boswell family, whose
great-grandfather was called Tyso Noname. When he was a
baby his mother took him to church to be christened. When
the minister asked her what name she had decided on for the
child, she replied: 'Tyso Jehovah Boswell,' but when told
that Jehovah could not be used and the reason why, she then
said: 'He shall have no other name but Tyso Noname
Boswell.'

On the Continent, where Gypsies frequently cross the
borders from one country to the next, they are likely to change
their official surnames as they go, which is easy enough when
they have to be translated anyway by the border officials
from the Cyrillic alphabet into the Roman, or from Turkish

into Greek. But, as with their Christian names, they may use quite different surnames amongst themselves.

Another favourite trick is to give officials a name which in Romany has a ribald or obscene meaning, so that whenever it is used by, say, the police or magistrates, the joke is on the *gorgio*.

In Britain, the *Rom* are more conventional with their surnames: they stick to the English names they first adopted for themselves on arriving here generations ago. In this way you can identify each family as belonging to a large 'clan'. The most common Gypsy surnames are:

Smith, Cooper, Boswell, Wood, Lee, Thorpe, Heron, Herne or Hearne, Locke, Lovell, Wilson, West, Buckley, Loveridge, Butler, Taylor, Buckland, Bunce, Chilcott, Draper, Gray, Pinfold, Reynolds, Shaw, Stanley, Worton, Young.

There is a strict and universal rule among the Romanies, that death, like birth, must always take place outside the caravan, otherwise the caravan would be considered *mookedo* (unclean or defiled). It may seem callous to take a dying man from his bed in the comfort of his caravan, and place him in a tent nearby for his last hours, but to the Romany, it is the right and proper thing to do.

If you look at the eighth photograph you can see a group of people outside the tent in which Mimi Rossetti, an Italian *phui dai* or female chief, lay dying. Notice the horror on the faces of the curious *gorgio* onlookers, and the grieving but resigned expression of the Gypsies. Marika, expected to be Mimi's successor, sits smoking her pipe in the middle of the group.

In some Romany tribes, all a man's possessions are destroyed when he dies, in a ritual burning of his caravan containing all his worldly possessions. We do not know the reason for this custom, but it may have originally been done for reasons of hygiene, or maybe even as a sign of the Romany's disregard for material goods. He has but few belongings because he needs so little for his way of life and is not interested in acquiring things for their own sake. The ritual burning seems to reflect his attitude towards the rightful purpose of these objects. His sons cannot expect to inherit anything from their father, which cuts out the bickering and ill-feeling which often accompanies a *gorgio* death. They have only the memory of him to help them through their lives, but he will almost certainly have prepared them well for the deliberately harsh life they lead. Gypsies greatly cherish the memories of their dead and recall them with enormous respect.

Although the fact of death is faced up to realistically, the grief felt by the family and clan is no less for all this. A wake (funeral lament) begins before death. The whole family gathers around the dying man or woman, and although their sorrow is usually fairly restrained while the person lives, immediately he dies there is an enormous display of grief. Men and women sob and wail, and on some occasions – say on the death of an important chief, or a child – the whole clan becomes almost insane with grief. Finally, they begin a rhythmic chanting, often of great beauty and poetry, which, at each death bed is both improvized and original, never being repeated in exactly the same way for anyone else.

This outward display of sorrow is very different from our own reaction to death, and perhaps it is healthier than our stiff-upper-lip attitude. We try to appear as brave and unaffected by death as possible, but perhaps it is more sensible to express grief than to smother it under a display of getting-on-with-life-as-best-we-can.

Romany relatives will fast from the time of death until the funeral is over, and often for quite a long period after that. At the same time they will not wash, shave, do their hair or dress up at all. A vigil is usually kept over the body until burial.

Romany funerals vary from country to country, and even from one tribe to another. The actual funeral service is just like our own, the coffin being buried in the nearest local cemetery, but various customs are observed in addition. Usually the family drop coins into the grave with the coffin, and sprinkle beer or wine over it. After the funeral, few Gypsies will return to the grave of the deceased. There is one tribe, however, called the Sinti, which visits the graves of its departed once a year on All Saints Day, when their wanderings make this possible. The tribe feasts near the grave and scatters some of its food and drink over it. Spilling drink on the ground at any time is a mark of respect for the dead observed by all Romanies.

Marriage, like christenings and funerals, is another important ceremony in a Gypsy's life. The form of marriage varies with different tribes, for instance, on the Continent the ancient practice of marriage-by-purchase is still followed, although it is becoming more and more symbolic. The custom is for the boy's father to call on the father of the girl, who pretends not to know anything of the proposed match. When the boy's father discloses the purpose of his visit, the other man will protest at the very idea of parting with his daughter! Both men will then praise their offspring to the skies, each extolling the virtues of his own child. When this little ceremony has gone on long enough, the father of the bride-to-be will settle on a price for his daughter. Then the young couple are brought together, and it is considered seemly for the daughter to show distress at leaving her family. The match is then announced to the rest of the tribe, and the marriage ceremony is held. The celebrations following this wedding are in true Romany style, though the lavishness of the feasting will depend on the wealth of the families concerned.

Another custom among some Continental Romanies is

marriage-by-abduction, in which the bride is virtually 'kid-napped' by her ardent suitor. Nowadays it is almost certainly 'abduction by consent', with the bride knowing all about it beforehand and being carried away with everyone's full approval.

The actual wedding ceremony usually consists of a public

agreement to the match by the parents and the young couple, and the eating of bread and salt. The head of the tribe officiates at the ceremony, and hands the broken pieces of bread, sprinkled with salt, to the bride and groom with the words, 'When you are tired of this bread and this salt, you'll be tired of one another'. The couple exchange portions before eating them. This ceremony takes place before the assembled families of the couple, usually in the open air at some specially chosen quiet spot.

In Britain, elopement is still occasionally practised. The couple disappear for a few weeks and when they return their parents are at first annoyed, but then welcome the match, and hold the marriage ceremony (*rommeripen*).

As with baptism, the church or registry office ceremony (when there is one) is of secondary importance to the Romany celebration. This is often quite simple and consists of the couple's publicly declared intention, and the joining of hands. There are reports, however, of far more elaborate and picturesque ceremonies.

In Dorothy Strange's book, *Born on the Straw*, which is the biography of a *gorgio* girl who married a Gypsy, there is a fascinating account of this couple's wedding.

All the groom's people had travelled in their wagons to meet up at a lonely spot in a wild part of Derbyshire. As evening drew in, and following a good plain meal of meat, fish or sausages, with bread and butter and tea, they gathered together around the big communal camp-fire. Dressed in their best clothes, the bride wearing all her necklaces and a colourful *joddakai*, the groom with a bright new *diklo*, the couple entered the assembled circle and went over to Old Jem, the head of the groom's family.

First, the groom was offered a bunch of twigs from which he chose only those woods from which he would be making pegs, skewers, holly rings, flower baskets and wooden shredded chrysanthemums for his wife to sell when she went hawking. These, the willow, holly, and elder twigs were laid on the ground, and the rest were thrown by Old Jem into the fire.

He then asked them if they wanted to be man and wife. When they said that they did, he took out his knife and with the tip of it he deftly nicked the groom's right wrist and the bride's left. When a trickle of blood began to show, the wrists were tied together and, palm to palm, their blood mingled, signifying that a life-long unity had been formed. On tying the first knot in the cord Old Jem said, 'This'll be so's ye'll be true an' faithful!' On tying a second knot he added, 'An' 'ere's 'opin' ye wears well!' And on the third he concluded, 'Lots of *chavis*!' (Children).

With their wrists still tied they jumped over the fire, then ran to the nearby stream into which they walked until their shoes were covered with water, symbolically showing that they would endure all perils together.

All that remained then was for the husband to give his wife the gold earrings that would be her greatest pride, this being the most sacred part of the wedding ritual as he fixed them gently to her ears. After a loving *choomia* (kiss) the singing and dancing began, and the beer started to flow.

This particular wedding took place in the 1950's. Nowadays, some or all of these customs are still observed by rural Gypsies. There is, too, an additional custom of leaping over a great bunch of furze, or broom, the Romany's flower, which is to ensure that the couple is blessed with plenty of children.

A Romany marriage lasts for life, and divorce is practically unheard of. The family unit is of supreme importance and although the children may be deprived of many things we would consider essential, they grow up happy and well-adjusted, with a family atmosphere of love and trust. The ages are not segregated as they often are in our society; old and young live naturally side-by-side and enjoy each other's company. The Gypsy approach to life is tough, physically, but mental illness is virtually unheard of. None of the pleasant or unpleasant things of life are ever hidden and this open, natural, way of life seems to make for healthy, well-balanced children and adults.

THREE

Crime and Punishment

Journalists and romantic novelists are fond of writing about Gypsy 'Kings' and 'Queens'. In fact, there are no such individuals, although the Gypsies themselves sometimes encourage the belief, so as to conceal the identity of their true leaders – the men who genuinely do have great powers of influence over them.

In each family group the chief or leader is the father or grandfather, and in a group of families forming a clan, there will be one elder accepted by general agreement as the over-all chief. This is not an hereditary responsibility, and he is elected for his wisdom, strength of character, and feeling for justice. These elders have great authority and hold enormous influence over their people. They are usually addressed, however, as *Kako*, or Uncle, and this friendly term emphasises the willing cooperation of the *Rom* regarding all matters relating to their law. Obedience to this is based not on fear, but on a deep awareness of the fact that within their tribal discipline lies their only course for survival. In Britain today, more than at any other time, there is little room for such individualists as the Romanies. They must be loyal to remain strong.

The female counterpart to '*Kako*', is '*Bibi*', or Auntie.

This is the *Phui Dai*, the wise old woman of the tribe. She wields great power, although it is of a more subtle nature than that of the chief. She will always be consulted in matters concerning the women or children, and she is also the expert in all occult matters. She is invariably a great personality and her influence is a very strong force in Romany life.

The standard Romany punishment from a parent is a box on the ears, or a good thrashing, and a grieved husband may even dole out the same punishment to his wife! Any major lapse from the Romany code of living is dealt with very severely by the *Kriss*, a periodic gathering of Romany elders, which is their equivalent of our court of law. At this *Kriss* all serious disputes amongst themselves are settled.

Without this system of law enforcement, the Romanies as a race would have disintegrated long ago. The *Kriss* makes sure that the Gypsy keeps to the rules of his race and so safeguards his unique way of life.

For this reason, enormous importance is attached to this periodic ceremony. To us, both the crimes and the punishments would seem strange. The *Rom* have their own, very workable scale of values, and their own way of treating offenders.

No true *Rom* would dream of reporting another of his people to the police. If, for some reason a matter *is* judged by the official law of the land, it will still be brought before the *Kriss* who will take absolutely no notice of what happened in the *gorgio* trial.

More than any other ceremony, the *Kriss* is kept strictly secret from all *gorgios*. From a very few reliable sources, we are able to build up a picture of what happens. The men who are old enough and wise enough to have achieved the required stature in life, gather together in a circle with the person presiding, called the *Krisnitori*, in the place of honour. All the younger men stand behind. They may listen but not take part. Women are not admitted to the *Kriss* at all, except as witnesses, with the exception of the *Phui Dai*, the senior woman of the tribe, whose opinion will be sought especially in regard to any matter concerning the women.

Each complaint is thrashed out amongst the elders, and no stone is left unturned to establish the truth. Matters brought up vary enormously but the most common are disputes and conflicts between families or groups, brawls followed by blows and wounds, jealousy with regard to business or trade, insults, and the non-observance of Romany laws, particularly that of *Mookedo*, which are taboos regarding cleanliness.

Theft within the tribe is rare. If it does occur, or if some other misdemeanour arises where a culprit must be found, there will be a *solakh*. This ceremony is held around a sort of altar made up of a makeshift altar-cloth (a *diklo* or scrap of cotton) hung over a stone. A candle burns, and on the cloth there may be photographs of their dead ones (whose spirits they believe guide them) and cut wild flowers. (Cut flowers are a symbol of premature death to the Romanies, who prefer to see them growing naturally.)

In this grave and tense atmosphere the culprit has a last chance to own up, and if he doesn't, each witness in turn comes up before the *Krisnitori*, or leader, and swears on oath. He or she is then interrogated closely, and conditionally cursed. The questions grow more complex and subtle, and the curses become more and more terrible. This form of third degree is charged with emotion, and is perhaps one of the most powerful traditions of the *Rom*. Nearly always the guilty person breaks down and confesses. As a Gypsy saying goes, 'Guilt can be forgiven, but it should never be hidden.'

The punishments naturally vary, but a death sentence has become very rare. The most dreaded sentence is banishment from the community. A beating, or other physical sentence, is another of the more extreme forms of punishment and can be violent and horrible. Many of the wrongdoers have to make amends in a material way, such as providing the wronged family with food for a couple of days.

After the *Kriss*, a feast or *pativ* is held in honour of anyone found not guilty. He drinks a toast and spills a little on the ground as a mark of respect for the dead, who have been responsible for guiding the *Kriss*. In some tribes the acquitted one will sing an account of the crime or offence, a sort of lament, whilst a woman dances and mimes the action, and all others present hum an accompaniment.

The harsh penalties inflicted on the guilty person, and the touching celebration for the innocent, brings to a fitting end this all-important ceremony. Together with the Romany's loyalty to his family and tribe, the *Kriss* is responsible for the great cohesion of the Romany people.

FOUR

Along the Road

Romanies take little account of birthdays. Apart, perhaps, from Christmas, the annual festivals are the horse fairs that are still held in different parts of Britain. The biggest and best-known is the one held in June at Appleby in Westmoreland, but there are many others. Gypsies may not now go to them all, but if there is a horse fair near where you live, look for them there. They have certainly attended recent fairs at Bromsgrove and Stow on the Wold.

On a Fair Day the Gypsies will wear all their finery, and set forth early in the morning to reach the town, with the money they've earned during the preceding weeks burning their pockets. They may or may not intend to do any actual horse-trading, but all who go intend to enjoy themselves.

Most towns where fairs are held have at least one shop which understands the needs of Gypsies, and here they can buy the small things they require. Similarly, there is usually one public house in each town which welcomes all 'travellers'. It is marked by a secret sign, known only to Gypsies.

Now that it is difficult for large groups of Romanies to travel the roads together, these fairs are good meeting-grounds for families who are forced to travel separately. The public house or *kichema* is the scene of lively reunions and the exchange of news. You may see large groups of Gypsies on these occasions, laughing and talking in high spirits. For some, these gatherings are the only time they use their Romany tongue. In doing so, they feel both a pride in their race, and a bond against the *gorgios*, from whom they can keep what secrets they choose.

Of course, the horse trade today does not compare with the youthful memories of the older Gypsies – the days when horses drew fine carriages, tradesmen's vans, carts, drays, canal barges, farmers' ploughs, and many other things. But so long as horses survive in any capacity, the Romanies will be around to deal in them, for they love horses more than any other animal, and have an almost uncanny affinity with them. A day at a horse fair is certainly a day to be enjoyed by them all!

The biggest and most famous gathering of Romanies, however, is not at a fair, but on a pilgrimage. This is at Saintes-Maries-de-la-Mer in France. On the 24th and 25th of May each year, hundreds of Romanies converge at this village on the coast of the Camargue in the south of France. They come not only from all over France, but from many parts of Europe, and even America.

Here in the little church at Saintes-Maries-de-la-Mer, there is a statue of Sara, the Kali. The meaning of her name is Sara, 'the dark woman', or Gypsy woman. Tradition has it that Sara, who was a chief of the Sinti tribe of Gypsies, living near the River Rhône, was present when three saints landed at Saintes-Maries-de-la-Mer soon after the death of Christ. The saints were the three Marys, Mary Salomé, Mary Jacobé and Mary Magdalene. As their boat neared the shore, Sara placed her dress on the sea, and using it as a raft went out to greet the saints and help them to land safely. The saints then baptised her, and she travelled around the Camargue collecting alms for her mistresses, whilst they preached the Gospel among the *gorgios* and the *Rom*.

This annual pilgrimage was originally instituted by the Catholic Church to commemorate the landing of the three Marys, and has been recorded since the fifteenth century. Since that time the Gypsies have gradually taken over the occasion as their own until today it is solely a Gypsy pilgrimage which has the full blessing of the Catholic Church.

A whole night's vigil is kept by the Romanies in the crypt of the church where there are two very old altars and the statue of Sara, the Kali.

One after the other, the Gypsies, especially the women, reverently kiss or stroke the statue, and hang up beside it a strip of cloth or small article of clothing. Finally, they touch the statue with small articles belonging to absent friends or relatives, or maybe a photograph, in order that they also may be blessed.

The following day there is a procession to the sea and here the statue of Sara is symbolically immersed in the water.

After these rituals, there follow, of course, the usual festivities.

Although most Romanies cannot read or write, and the Romany language has no written tradition, they do have a wonderful method of sign language called *patrin*.

As a family wends its way through the countryside it leaves signs for other Romanies on the road. One of the most useful is the sign showing which way it has travelled and this is represented by a cross, the longest arm of which shows the way the caravan went. This is especially useful when the police move on a caravan at short notice while one or more of the family is away hawking or working.

There are other, more complicated signs made with leaves (*patrin* means leaf in Romany), twigs, branches, and grass tied in a certain way, usually on the left-hand side of the road. A few wisps of grass tied to the branch of a roadside tree can have an important meaning to a fellow Romany. They also use scraps of food, horse hair, feathers, pieces of trimmed wood, stones, scraps of cloth (red indicating male, and white, female); the manner of placing these various natural items, has a specific meaning for Gypsies. Furthermore, each tribe has its own personal sign, so you can see that with all these components quite complicated messages may be left along the roadside for the next group of gypsies.

In addition to this, there is a set of symbols which can be chalked or carved outside a farm or house for the information of subsequent Gypsy callers.

Here is a list of some of their signs, although the meanings

cannot be guaranteed to be entirely accurate since naturally they are highly secret:

☩	Here they give nothing
╪	Beggars badly received
◯	Generous people
◉	Very generous people and friendly to Gypsies
◉̲	Here Gypsies are regarded as thieves
///	We have already robbed this place
△	You can tell fortunes with cards
≋	The mistress wants a child
⚡	She wants no more children
⊖	Old woman died recently
⊙	Old man died recently
⊙	At loggerheads about an inheritance
△	Master just died
⊿	Mistress is dead
⊖	Mistress is dissolute

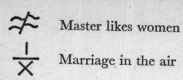   Master likes women

Marriage in the air

The last ten may seem to be somewhat useless information, but in fact if a Gypsy woman whilst out hawking, has picked up any such pieces of information, they can be extremely useful to another Gypsy calling later. She may indeed have excellent 'second sight', but if, armed with such information, she can impress the lady of the house with some immediate fortune-telling before getting the opportunity to look at her palm, she renders her far more gullible to any tricks she may want to try!

FIVE

Living off the Land

Living so close to nature, the Romanies naturally have an unrivalled understanding of all plant and animal life. Their understanding of animals is profound, but it is not a romantic sympathy, as many wild animals and birds are caught only to be eaten! In fact the Romanies are no keepers of pets as such. What need have they of these when there is such a rich variety of animal life on their doorsteps? Apart from caged songbirds and perhaps an odd bantam or two, the only other domestic animals you will see around a Gypsy camp are dogs, and these you will quickly realize are not kept for sentimental reasons: they are indispensable to the Romany for the protection of his caravan and the hunting of his food.

Lurchers, as the coursing dogs are called, are very valuable to their Gypsy owners. They are a cross-breed of greyhound with either collie, Scots deerhound or Irish wolfhound. The aim is to produce a dog with the speed of the greyhound but with a rough coat and more intelligence. These dogs are carefully trained to hunt silently for rabbits and hares. They are careful to keep themselves concealed when strangers are near and will often make their own way back to the camp with their kill. In fact, a good lurcher will go quite alone into a field, catch a fine meal and deliver it up without its master having committed trespass at all! Of course, a well-trained dog is highly prized and fabulous tales are told amongst the *Rom* to illustrate the skill of their own particular dog. Needless to say, a *gorgio* will never be able to obtain one of the puppies as they are kept very strictly within 'the family'.

The Romany is supreme master of poaching. He never carries, let alone owns, a gun. He manages to catch exactly what he wants by much better methods.

His intimate knowledge of the animals' habits, plus his inherited skill help him to construct simple traps, snares and baits that are far more effective than those of the clumsy *gorgio*.

The Gypsy actually invented the idea of artifical baits for fishing! Over a hundred and sixty years ago the Romanies used little wooden fish decorated with tufts of coloured feathers, in the middle of which hooks were concealed. They also invented the artificial fly for trout fishing. In addition they use magical baits such as 'Magic nutmeg' or 'Radioactive ball'. These consist of gums from resinous plants or stones coated with sweet-smelling oils.

A Romany can, however, catch a trout or salmon without a rod or a net, using only his hands. He is so still, quiet and patient that a bird, fish or animal doesn't know of his presence until it is too late. In this way he is able to catch a pheasant with a special hand-made whip, flicking it around the bird's neck, or, in the absence of a dog to help him, he can catch and instantly kill a rabbit or hare with a sharp blow of his stick or *cosh* on the back of its head. In all cases these manoeuvres are carried out in uncanny silence.

Of course a Romany will not call this stealing. The whole concept of theft is a *gorgio* one. To his way of thinking he is not taking the property of others: he is only claiming his rightful share of the fruits of the earth, the birds of the air, or

God's creatures generally. He doesn't understand the law of property at all!

Romanies are essentially foragers. At one time they must have lived entirely on what food they could find in the countryside, and even today food from the land forms the larger part of a country Gypsy's diet.

As we have already seen they are expert poachers, and since they love to eat meat it is by this method that most of it is obtained. Because of their special regard for horses, they will never eat horse meat, even on the Continent where it is customary amongst the *gorgios*. Nor would they eat the meat of a dog or cat. But they do consume many other animals and birds that we would not dream of touching.

Hedgehog (*hotchi-witchi*) is a popular delicacy amongst the *Rom*. On the Continent hedgehogs are encased in clay and baked in the fire. When cooked, the clay is chipped away and the hedgehog's prickles sticking to the clay come away, too. Then the entrails are removed and the meat eaten with a little salt, and lots of wild garlic and wild fresh herbs.

In England the *hotchi-witchi* is skinned first, split down the back, flattened out, cleaned in salt water, then roasted on a spit over the fire. The meat is basted in its own fat and is said to be delicious – rather like pheasant or grouse.

Another delicacy is snails (*bouries*). Towards the end of the year large ones may be found clustered together in the bottom of a tree stump or in the cracks of a wall. They are washed, and either roasted, or else dipped in boiling water, then prized out, dipped in salt and eaten with bread and butter, and strong tea. A soup is also made with snails. It is called *bouri zimmen*.

The Romany's breakfast is a simple meal of bread, possibly cheese, and lots of strong tea. His other meal, supper, consists generally of a stew, followed again by tea.

The large stewpot can contain a remarkable selection of meat quite apart from the usual beef, lamb or pork which, when there's enough money, the gypsy may buy from a butcher's shop. The Gypsies squatting around the fire in the evening can equally well expect to fork out a piece of rabbit, hare, pheasant, chicken, partridge or grey squirrel. Many small wild birds are also put into the pot: blackbirds,

thrushes, lapwings, fieldfares, pigeons and moorhens. Even cygnet (young swan) is not unknown if it can be obtained. It tastes best if caught just before the brown plumage becomes flecked with white.

All Romany stews are enhanced with the addition of vegetables, nettles, mushrooms, truffles, the fungi called blue legs, and a mixture of wild fresh herbs.

Another, though rare, meal would consist of the cured

hams of a badger. Apparently it is difficult to distinguish the taste of this dish from lean bacon.

They are not great eaters of sweet things, but puddings, jellies, pickles, drinks and jams are made from the blackberries and rose-hips which they gather from the hedgerow.

Gypsies tend to smoke a lot – perhaps because food is not always plentiful. Even the women, especially the older ones, can be seen puffing away at a clay pipe! In hard times, when tobacco can't be afforded, they smoke dried oak leaves. Dried coltsfoot leaves are also smoked and are said to be good for the throat and lungs.

Romanies love their beer from the *kichema* or public house, but many still make their own beer and wine. Excellent beer can be brewed with nettles, and how cheaply they can make wine from all sorts of wild plants: dandelions, blackberries, elderberries, elderflowers, rose-hips, balm, camomile, cowslips, coltsfoot and so on.

Another favourite drink is herb tea. The Gypsies make this both as a refreshing drink and as a medicine, but more about this in the next chapter.

SIX

Recipes and Cures

Herbs are used a great deal in Romany medicine. The old Gypsy women know the healing properties of all the herbs and plants, and even use the bark of certain trees. This knowledge and skill is passed down through the generations. The 'recipes' have to be learnt by heart, since few can read or write.

Romanies also drink herb teas, partly as cures and partly as a form of preventive medicine. They say that tea made from mugwort or cowslips helps you to sleep. So does thyme, which is also good for chest complaints. Tea made from dandelion leaves or the flowers of centaury is good for 'purifying the blood' and sage tea is taken to ease kidney troubles. Coltsfoot tea eases throat and chest complaints, and tea brewed with meadowsweet flowers prevents diarrhoea. Camomile is reputed to be good for nervous headaches, and tea made from the dried leaves of balm will act in the same way. Nettle tea is very popular and is good for high blood-pressure. It will also sooth an ulcerated mouth or sore throat. Catmint tea is good to take if you feel a cold coming on, and mint tea is an aid to digestion.

Not all herbal remedies are medicines to be swallowed, or

rubbed on as a lotion. Sometimes the leaves or roots of a plant are worn as a charm to ward off illnesses, but more of this in a later chapter.

Because of the healthy, natural, out-door life they lead, Gypsies are not greatly troubled by ill-health. However, here are examples of the way they tackle both slight disorders and more serious complaints when they do occur, and many are the *gorgios* who have had occasion to be grateful for an old Gypsy woman's cure!

ASTHMA   (1) Prepare either an infusion or, preferably, a decoction of coltsfoot. (An *infusion* is made like tea, by pouring on boiling water. A *decoction* consists of boiling the herb in water until it has been reduced to about half its original quantity.)

(2) Boil 1 oz of sweet chestnut leaves in 1½ pints of water for 10 minutes. Strain off the water and add ½ oz honey and ½ oz glycerine. Take first thing in the morning and last thing at night.

(3) Prepare an infusion of thyme.

(4) Smoke dried coltsfoot leaves in a pipe!

BLOOD PRESSURE   Boil 1 oz of chopped stinging nettles in 1 pint of water for five minutes. Strain, boil liquid again, then bottle. Take two tablespoons, three times a day.

BOILS   Bruise some leaves of cuckoo-pint and apply frequently to the boil until it has disappeared.

The pain of a boil can be eased by holding over it alder leaves which have been dipped in hot water.

BRONCHITIS   Make horehound tea, or an infusion of red clover, sweetened with honey. Take a wineglassful three times a day.

BRUISES (1) Pound the dried leaves of pot marjoram into a powder, mix with honey and rub on to the bruise. It will ease the pain and remove the discolouration.

(2) Oil made from sweet marjoram can be rubbed on sprains and bruises with great effect.

CATARRH Soak dried horse-chestnut leaves in a solution of 1 oz of saltpetre to $\frac{1}{4}$ pint of warm water. Dry the leaves again, rub into a powder and burn, inhaling the fumes.

CHILBLAINS (1) Slice a raw potato and cover with salt. Leave overnight, then rub a slice on the chilblain, leaving it to dry on the skin. Apply as often as possible and the chilblain will soon disappear.

(2) Dip a slice of lemon or onion in salt and rub on the chilblain.

(3) To 2 pints of water in which parsnips have been boiled without salt, add 1 tablespoon of powdered alum, stirring well. Soak the chilblains for twenty minutes then let the solution dry on. Use this solution frequently until chilblains have quite disappeared.

(4) For broken chilblains, bake an unpeeled turnip in the oven. Cut it open and lay a piece as hot as you can bear over the affected place. Afterwards, dress the chilblain with zinc ointment or Vaseline on a clean rag.

COLDS (1) Prepare a decoction of nettle leaves mixed with honey to make a syrup. Take 1 teaspoonful before going to bed.

(2) Make an infusion of mugwort, camomile flower, coltsfoot or ground ivy with wood sage, and take at bedtime.

(3) Stew barberry berries with a little water until soft, strain and add three parts water to one of juice. Drink hot at night.

CORNS (1) Put some young ivy leaves in a jar and cover with vinegar. Leave for 24 hours. Then each day take a leaf and tie it around the corn. This will stop the pain and in two to four weeks the corn will come away.

(2) Put a mother-of-pearl button in an eggcup and cover with lemon juice. Cover the eggcup and leave for three days. By then the button should have dissolved, leaving a thick creamy mixture. Paint this on the corns and leave for two days. Then soak the foot in hot water, when both covering and corns should come away!

COUGHS (1) Drink eyebright, coltsfoot or borage tea, or swallow a tablespoonful of an infusion of agrimony four times a day.

(2) Prepare a decoction of coltsfoot leaves, with honey and lemon juice added. Take a wineglassful three times a day.

(3) Gather together 2 oz of coltsfoot leaves, 1 oz of hyssop, 1 oz of black horehound, 1 oz of lump ginger. Put all ingredients into 2 quarts of water and boil down to 1 quart. Drink cold as desired.

(4) For a hard cough, put a tablespoonful of vinegar and a tablespoonful of sugar into the beaten white of an egg. Take at bedtime.

(5) For a bad cough make a pint of syrup from sugar and water. Add 1 oz of fresh red clover leaves. Boil, strain, and bottle, corking tightly. Take a teaspoonful two or three times a day.

(6) Dissolve $\frac{1}{4}$ oz of black liquorice in $\frac{1}{4}$ pint of white vinegar. Add 2 oz of honey, and when the mixture is cool, add the juice of a lemon. Take a teaspoonful as necessary.

(7) Stew black cherries in a little water, strain well and add honey and lemon juice. Take a teaspoonful as necessary.

(8) Scrape half a cupful of horseradish and add enough vinegar to just cover it. Keep pressing down. Leave for

twenty-four hours. Add a tablespoonful of glycerine and mix. Take half a teaspoonful in a wineglass of hot water.

CUTS (1) Romany Balm can be bought from herbalists, but here is the recipe: 4 oz of the fat from a pig's kidney, 1 oz of cuttings from the 'frog' of the horse hoof, 1 houseleek, 1 oz of scrapings from the bark of the elder tree. Place all together in an enamelled pan placed over a slow heat. Stir while the fat is sizzling, and allow to simmer for half-an-hour. Strain into a clean jar, allow to set and keep covered.

You can use this ointment on any cuts, sores or bruises.

(2) Gather elder flowers when they are open. Lay them in home-cured, saltless lard and heat very, very, slowly so that all the juice comes out and penetrates the lard. Allow to cool, and pot.

(3) Pick elderberries while still green, wash well, put in a stone jar and cover with camphorated oil. Set a plate on top of the jar and stand it in a pan of boiling water for four hours. Strain through muslin and put into jars.

(4) Take a handful of the herb frogbit, wash it very thoroughly and put in a jar with ½ lb of clarified lard. Stand the jar in a pan of boiling water and simmer for two hours, stirring often.

This ointment is a fine healer of all cuts and bruises, spots and broken pimples.

DEPRESSION (1) Take a handful of wood-sage, put in a jug and pour 1 pint of boiling water over it. Cover with a cloth and leave for twenty-four hours. Drink a wineglassful first thing in the morning before breakfast and another three days later. The water must not be strained off from the herb, because the infusion must grow stronger. The three-day interval is most important in this cure.

(2) Infuse 1 oz of dried or fresh hops in 1 pint of boiling water. Cover closely, leave until cold and do not strain. Take a wineglassful three times a day, an hour before meals.

FAILING MEMORY!   Make an infusion of 1 oz of eyebright to 1 pint of water. Let it cool, strain it, and take a wineglassful three times a day.

GUMBOILS AND ULCERS IN MOUTH   (1) Take a dried fig, put it on a saucer and cover with milk. Place another saucer on top and put into the oven. In twenty minutes the milk should be absorbed and the fig swollen up. Cut a slice from the middle of the fig and place it on the painful area as hot as can be borne. Repeat this treatment for as long as necessary.

(2) Use cold blackberry leaf tea as a mouth wash or simply chew the young leaves.

HAY FEVER   (1) Take ¼ oz each of centaury, horehound, red sage, vervain and yarrow. Mix well in a pint of cold water. Bring to the boil and simmer for fifteen minutes. Strain, and take half a teacupful four times a day. Half dose for children.

HEADACHE   (1) Prepare a decoction of willow bark.

(2) Make an infusion of dried lime flowers and drink hot. If possible lie down for half-an-hour, after which the cure will be complete and lasting.

(3) For a nervous headache, make an infusion of the flowery tops of rosemary.

(4) For a severe headache put a pinch of dried marjoram into a cup and half fill with boiling water. Cover and allow to draw, then drink whilst hot.

INFLUENZA   Prepare a decoction of ½ oz of elder flowers and 1 oz of peppermint herbs with 1 pint of boiling water. Sweeten with sugar or treacle and drink the mixture hot at bedtime.

Here are two preventatives to colds and 'flu:

(a) Take 15 drops of essence of cinnamon on a lump of sugar.

(b) Mix together in a bottle ¼ oz formalin and 4 oz Eau-de-Cologne. Rub a little on the palms of the hands and inhale through the nose.

INSECT BITES (1) Rub on lemon juice or salt, the bruised leaves of houseleek, or pimpernel.

(2) To prevent stings and bites from wasps, horse flies and mosquitos, make an infusion of feverfew. When cool, sponge on to exposed skin.

INSOMNIA (1) Sleep on a pillow stuffed with hops.

(2) Make cowslip tea, leave to stand for five minutes, and take on going to bed. A tiny pinch of isinglass in this will rest a weary brain.

(3) Eat raw lettuce leaves just before going to bed.

LARYNGITIS (1) Boil 1 oz of blackcurrant leaves in 1 pint of water. Strain and bottle. Take a tablespoonful two or three times a day.

(2) Obtain the juice of a cabbage by boiling it in very little water. Mix honey in the juice and take as desired.

(3) Drink an infusion of red sage.

RHEUMATISM (1) Eat celery every day. If fresh celery is unobtainable, stew celery seed in milk, strain, and take three times a day between meals. This is also a good cure for lumbago and sciatica.

(2) Make a decoction of 1 oz of dandelion root in 1½ pints water. Strain, cool and take a wineglassful twice a day.

The above methods will cure rheumatism quite quickly it it is caught in its early stages. Prolonged treatment is necessary in chronic cases, and for use in the meantime, here are two simple poultices which will relieve the pain.

(3) Pour enough boiling water over a handful of hops until they are quite soaked. Wrap in a piece of muslin and place on the affected part.

(4) Wrap dried marjoram in muslin and heat in the oven. Place over the area of pain.

SHOCK   Prepare an infusion of either camomile flowers or balm, using 1 oz of herbs to 1 pint of water. Take cold, a wineglassful three times a day.

SPLINTERS   The Romany way of drawing out splinters in the flesh is by filling a narrow-necked bottle with hot water and emptying it again when the glass is as hot as possible. The neck of the bottle is then placed over the splinter, and as the bottle cools down a vacuum is created which sucks the splinter to the surface. They are always very careful to handle the bottle with a cloth, and not to get the bottle so hot that it cracks or breaks!

WARTS   There are several cures for warts, but the quickest one is to rub on the juice from a dandelion leaf. Apply a drop of this milky substance each day and the wart will soon turn black, then disappear.

This is only a small selection of Romany cures. It seems there is not an ailment known which cannot be relieved or cured by one herb or another. For a really comprehensive guide to Romany medicine you should read *The Romany Way to Health* by Charles Bowness, published by Thorsons Publishers Ltd, or *The Roots of Health* by Leon Petulengro, published by Souvenir Press and Pan Books Ltd.

As you would expect, if a Romany is an expert at curing his fellow men and maintaining an astonishing degree of good health, he is equally skilled in treating his horses. And of course it is only a short step from 'treating' them to horse faking, that is, disguising a horse's faults rather than actually curing them, in order to sell the animal.

A horse can successfully be cured of horse 'flu by making a

decoction of dried ash bark and blackberry leaves, adding to this previously boiled wheat and oats, rosehips, chopped onion and black treacle, and boiling it all together.

For constipation a horse is given salted meat juice, and to

make the animal urinate, he is given a handful of grass mixed with paprika.

To improve the breathing of a broken-winded horse, he is given lard and starch, or henbane and elderberries. This, however, is only a temporary cure, lasting just long enough for the animal to be sold!

A glandered horse can be disguised for a while by stuffing its nose with nettles an hour or so before offering it for sale. When the plug is removed, it is accompanied by a great quantity of mucus. The nostrils are then washed and he is ready to be shown.

Likewise, holes can be bored into the horse's teeth and filled with rosemary, to make his breath sweet. A horse's teeth are sometimes 'bishoped', that is, shortened with a hacksaw to make it appear younger.

In order to make a horse appear mettlesome and hold his tail nicely, some Romanies will put a piece of ginger into his bottom. They can also excite a horse and make him lively by pricking him gently with a hedgehog, just before showing him at a fair!

Then there is the old trick of rattling pebbles in a bucket under the animal's nose until he goes almost crazy. If this is done several times, it is only necessary, when selling him, to show him a bucket from a distance, and the oldest horse will prance about like a spirited young thing.

SEVEN

Tricks and Gypsy Magic

From the very earliest records we have of the Gypsies, we know that they have always been regarded with a mixture of fascination and fear. Their way of life, so very different from that of the *gorgios*, their wild and colourful appearance, and above all, their 'magic', both genuine and faked, has lent them an aura of mystery. This suits the Gypsies excellently, as they have no particular wish to be on familiar or friendly terms with us. In their eyes, the majority of *gorgios* are fools, who waste time, energy, and life itself on petty bureaucracy, the amassing of material possessions, over-eating, and generally leading a totally unnatural way of life. The Gypsies' greatest sport is (and always has been) that of hoodwinking the *gorgios*!

So it is not surprising that they should use their reputation for occult powers to trick gullible people in a purely physical, or non-occult, way. There are countless examples of tricks to play on the *gorgios* which the Romany's lively imagination has conjured up.

From early accounts of Gypsies in Europe we have the tale of a certain Gypsy who stole a sheep, and putting it into a sack, offered to sell it to a butcher. The butcher told the Gypsy he was asking too much money for it and walked on.

The Gypsy took the sheep from the sack and put in its place one of his small sons. He then ran after the butcher and offered him not only the sheep but the sack as well for a good price. The butcher agreed, paid the money and took home his purchase. Imagine the butcher's horror when, on opening the sack, out jumped a little boy, who of course lost no time in running away, taking the sack with him!

Another typical story dating from the early seventeenth century is of a Gypsy who sold pigs, which, he claimed, he had changed from bundles of hay. He always warned the buyer never to wash these animals. But after the next rainfall the buyer would invariably find bundles of hay in the sty – the Gypsy meanwhile having regained his porkers and moved on to resell them in the next town!

There are countless such stories. In the early days of the Romanies' appearance in Europe, not only were their Eastern magical powers wondered at, but their knowledge of herbal remedies gave them a reputation as healers; and skills such as those of the Gypsy show people – acrobats, ventriloquists, conjurors, and trainers of performing animals – were thought to be acts of sorcery or magic. If a bear, monkey, dog or goat took around a bowl for contributions, the crowd often imagined it was a person who had temporarily changed his form. Very often Gypsies were imprisoned or burned on suspicion of being witches.

Even today, a Romany has many ways of deceiving a *gorgio* with 'mock magic'. Not so very long ago Gypsy women had a favourite swindle. In the course of conversation whilst hawking, a Gypsy would find out about a housewife with some jewellery or savings put away. The Gypsy would win the woman's confidence by first of all telling her fortune – being remarkably accurate about the past and present, and giving helpful information and advice about the future, craftily adding at the end the possibility of the woman becoming very rich. Perhaps over a cup of tea, the Gypsy would

casually ask if the woman had heard that gold draws gold.
She would go on to explain that if she would wrap her savings
or jewellery in a cloth and bury them in the ground, she, the
Gypsy, would utter a magic spell over them, and if the woman
would leave the bundle in the ground for a month, the riches

would multiply. If the woman was foolish enough to believe
this, and do as the Gypsy said, you can imagine what she
really found on digging up the bundle one month later. By
this time the Gypsy would have put many miles between the
lady's house and her caravan!

But although the Romanies are quick to take advantage of
the impressionable *gorgio*, you must not imagine that there is
no foundation for their reputation of 'making magic'.

Of course we now know that skills born of long practice

and much patience are the making of the animal-trainer, conjuror and ventriloquist. And we know that their skills with herbs are the result of knowledge gained by generations of Romanies who lived so close to nature that they were able to observe minutely the effects of taking the various plants by which they were surrounded all their lives. A chemical analysis of many of their cures might prove that they simply contain nature's equivalents of the modern drugs we buy at chemist shops.

But what of their skill at what we call the occult sciences? They are remarkably good at astrology and palmistry, and telling fortunes by crystal-gazing and cards. Admittedly, not every Gypsy woman who sets herself up as a fortune-teller genuinely possesses these gifts, but an astonishing number of Romanies seem to.

It would also be foolish to ignore their powers of making charms or curses. They might just prove to be genuine!

There are a few charms for you to use against pain. Dock seeds, gathered when ripe should be put into a small muslin bag and worn around the left arm. This old Gypsy charm is said to be particularly effective against pain suffered by women and girls. Burdock seeds in a little muslin bag, worn around the neck, should keep rheumatism away. A root of vervain sewn into a little bag of red silk and worn around the neck is said to be a good cure for all lung troubles, such as bronchitis, asthma, and so forth. They say that this last charm is particularly effective for those people born under the sign of Taurus or Libra, and as the same charm is used for neutralizing evil wished upon you, it would be a useful one to try!

Anyone wishing to be beautiful, healthy and happy, should try wearing a sachet of the roots and leaves of the lemony-scented herb, balm, next to the heart!

The Gypsies of central Europe still make amulets and talismans by drawing or carving symbols on wooden discs, shells, stones or fossils. These symbols consist of stars, moons, flowers, birds and a variety of lines and dots which would look quite meaningless to us.

A few old Romany women are reputed to be witches — some practising white magic and some practising black. The black witches are supposed to have been chosen, as young girls, by demons visiting them at night. It is considered to be very fortunate for a girl to be chosen in this way. She must spend a long while mastering her craft from the elders, and the sort of evil spells she will learn to cast will cause her enemies suffering. For one such spell, she may make a model in melted candle-wax of the person in question, and attach it to a piece of the victim's clothing, hair or finger-nail. She will then prick the model with a needle nine times, and thus cast her evil spell.

Another spell consists of watering a branch of weeping-willow for nine days, saving the water each time. Then this water is poured on the threshold of the victim's home to bring him sorrow and anguish.

The ingredients for evil spells and potions are always nasty or rotten things, such as mouldy breadcrumbs, manure, snake-skins, powdered beetles and toads, saliva and so on.

A white witch is instructed in her art from infancy, by her mother and grandmother. *Her* magical powers are put to a far pleasanter use! She will have the ability to help and protect her people and she is especially able to do this because she is not distracted by the mechanical, routine or material-istic aspects of *gorgio* lives. She is able to be more aware of the natural world, and is therefore sensitive to wavelengths or vibrations which perhaps the majority of us no longer perceive.

Crystal-gazing is a magic art requiring this form of sensi-tivity, or extra-sensory perception (ESP) as it is sometimes called. Whilst this power flows through the Gypsy, she is in a trance and needs the crystal ball only for the purpose of focusing her attention. In this trance-like state the white witch is able to see future or past events and so help to guide her fellow Gypsies.

Such sensitivity, or intuition, is also needed to some degree in successful palmistry or card reading, but in addition these two arts have to be learned.

EIGHT

Reading Palms

Palmistry, unlike crystal-gazing, has to be learnt. It is based on information about the human palm amassed over centuries. We know that every hand-print in the world is unique; indeed thumb and fingerprints are widely used by the police as an infallible means of identification. It is not so strange, then, that the shape of the hands and fingers, and the lines on the palms should reflect our individuality, and since our actions, past and future, depend on our individual reaction to circumstances, it is perhaps not surprising that many people, including Gypsies, believe that future tendencies can be read on the palm.

Here's how palmistry is said to work. If a person is right-handed, his left hand will indicate all the possible trends in his life – his scope and potential as a human being. His right hand shows more specifically what he has already achieved – whether he has developed or neglected his talents and characteristics. With a left-handed person, of course, this order is reversed. Contrary to the practice adopted by most palmists, a Romany will read the left palm with only occasional reference to the right.

When reading a palm, a Romany will take three things

into account. Firstly, the general shape of the hand; secondly, the bumps or mounts on the palm; and lastly, the lines. Have a look at *your* hand as you read this section and see how you score.

THE SHAPE

The shape of the hand can be divided roughly into seven types:

1. *The Elementary Hand*   This hand is rather unusual. It has a large palm with short fingers. The thumb is particularly short and turned back.

This is the hand of a person having little or no manual or intellectual abilities and it is rare to find it amongst civilized peoples.

2. *The Spatulate Hand*   This is usually a rather large hand, but its main characteristic is that the ends of the fingers are broad.

People with this shaped hand will be practical, adventurous, capable, and above all, active. They will enjoy travel and are not easily discouraged.

3. *The Conical Hand*   This is a graceful hand with tapering fingers.

The owner will be impetuous and cheerful, with plenty of artistic sensibility, tactful, tolerant, and rather easily influenced. If the hand is slightly plump and soft, the person will be inclined to laziness.

4. *The Square Hand*   The palm of this hand is square and the fingers are almost squared-off at the tips.

It is the hand of a methodical, steady, conventional and practical person. He likes everything to be organized and will work hard for what he believes in.

5. *The Philosophical Hand*   This one is a long, slim hand. The fingers may end with a square, pointed or conical

Prince Gypsy Lee with his dog

A Gypsy man making artificial flowers from shavings. The
flowers will be dyed in pots over the fire

An old Gypsy woman smoking her pipe

A Gypsy man and his daughter in the Vale of Evesham; he is
making pegs

A decorated Gypsy caravan

A group of Gypsy children

French Gypsies touching the statue of their patron saint, Sarah. The statue is carried in procession through the streets of Saintes Maries de la Mer once a year and to touch it is thought to bring good luck

Italian Gypsies keeping vigil outside the tent of their dying queen

shape, but are always bony-looking and have knotted joints.

This hand indicates a thinker; a person who approaches all situations intellectually and is more inclined to contemplate than act. His knowledge will be considerable, though he will probably never be rich in a material sense.

6. *The Pointed Hand* Sometimes called the Psychic Hand, this is a slim, graceful hand, with smooth joints and pointed finger-tips.

It is the hand of an idealist, and a creative, artistic person. Inclined to be physically delicate, this person is intuitive and interested in religion or spiritual pursuits.

7. *The Mixed Hand* The most common type of hand, in which two or more types are combined.

Each mixed hand must be judged individually, for one aspect will modify the significance of another in this type of hand. The owner will be versatile and adaptable, although this could apply either to a shallow, easily-influenced person, or a talented all-rounder.

THE THUMB

The thumb is the most significant of all the digits to a Romany. Its shape and size will either reinforce or modify other aspects found in the hand or palm.

If the thumb reaches the first joint of the index, or forefinger, it is of average length. A long thumb indicates considerable willpower and influence over others, whilst a shorter thumb denotes correspondingly less willpower.

If the thumb bends back too far it indicates a weak-willed, ineffectual person. If, when the thumb is spread away from the other fingers, a wide angle is produced, it shows warmth and generosity. If the angle is narrow, the owner is cautious and perhaps greedy.

The thumb is divided into three parts or phalanges. These indicate love, will and logic. The first phalange from the tip to the middle joint represents willpower; the second, reasoning ability; and the third, which is actually a part of the palm, represents love and sympathy. The relative lengths of these three phalanges indicate the guiding force in the life of the owner.

If the thumb has a 'waist' it is a sign of diplomacy and sympathy. If the joint is knotty it shows an analytical mind; and if smooth, impulsiveness.

THE NAILS

The Romany palmist will examine the shape of both thumb and finger nails.

Long and slim – artistic, calm nature
Short – critical, impulsive
Broad – inclined to be interfering
Thick – lazy
Hard – plenty of stamina
Wedge-shaped – sensitive

THE MOUNTS

The next part of the palm to be examined is 'the mounts', that is the fleshy bumps on the palm. Each one is named after a planet, and bears the significance associated with each of the particular planets.

Mount of Venus   This has already been mentioned as the third phalange of the thumb, indicating love, affection and sympathy.

If it is well developed it denotes a kind-hearted generous person with a love of beauty and comfort. Overdevelopment suggests a temperamental person who is over-sensuous and

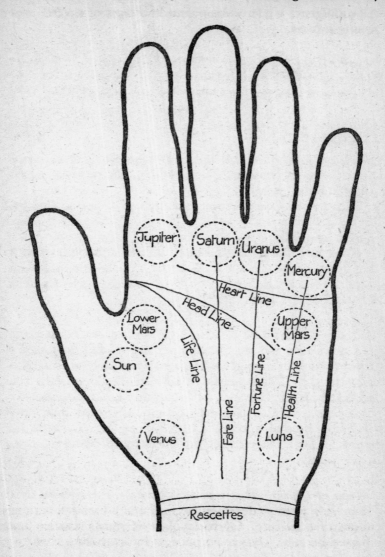

self-indulgent. Underdevelopment is a sign of a cold, un-
feeling subject.

Mount of Apollo (or Sun)   This is just above the Mount of
Venus. It denotes personal reputation and success, though in
a woman it may apply to effort devoted to her family.

Overdeveloped, it shows aggression and abusiveness;
underdeveloped, reticence.

Mount of Jupiter - This is the pad below the first or index
finger, and it indicates happiness in life and marriage,
ambition and pride.

If overdeveloped it shows conceit, and if flat, it shows a
lack of ambition and personal dignity – a person who prefers
a humdrum life.

A vertical line on this mount indicates success; a cross, a
happy marriage; and a star, fame. If the mount is placed
near to the second finger the subject will have an interest in
mystical or religious matters.

Mount of Saturn   This is at the base of the second finger and
is rarely overdeveloped. When it is it shows a morbid attitude
towards life. An average development shows a quiet, straight-
forward life. If it is positioned towards the ring finger this
indicates artistic interests, sentimentality and melancholy.

A short, vertical line on this mount means luck; two
indicate unusual success. Crossed lines show a need for
solitude, and a star shows the necessity for taking care of
one's health.

Mount of Uranus   This mount is beneath the ring or third
finger. An average development indicates a friendly, curious,
industrious nature. Overdeveloped it shows avarice and
big-headedness. Underdeveloped, it indicates meanness.

Mount of Mercury   The pad beneath the little finger is ruled by this planet which is associated with communication, intuition, eloquence and the ability to succeed.

A well developed Mount of Mercury then, will indicate a popular person – cheerful and friendly, practical, clear-thinking, talented, and successful in whatever walk of life he follows. Overdevelopment will suggest talkativeness and possibly deceit; and underdevelopment, inability to express ideas, and a life lacking purpose.

A single vertical line on this mount means wealth. Two or three lines show many useful interests. Four vertical lines is the sign of a doctor or a nurse, and more than four lines shows the person is talkative and careless about money. A cross shows tact, and a square, good business judgement.

The Mounts of Mars   There are two Mounts of Mars. Upper Mars is situated on the outside edge of the palm, beneath the Mount of Mercury, and Lower Mars is on the inside edge between the Mount of Jupiter and the Mount of Apollo. They both indicate courage, either mental or physical, but in Upper Mars it takes an active form and in Lower Mars a passive. Well balanced, and normally developed they show a brave, calm, persevering nature. Abnormally large, they show great courage and tenacity, or if the rest of the hand supports it, they could indicate a cruel, abusive temperament. Underdeveloped, they suggest lack of self-restraint, and a cowardly, defensive nature.

A square on Lower Mars is the sign of a poised person with a quick brain, and if there is a cross on Upper Mars it shows a quarrelsome nature.

Mount of Luna (or Moon)   This is on the bottom corner of the hand (the same side as the little finger). The Moon controls the imagination and temperament.

A mount of good average development shows a gentle

person with a poetic imagination and a developed sense of beauty. Lack of development means a lack of these qualities, little romantic feeling and a tendency to hardness. Over-development could mean the owner is ruled by his imaginings or even delusions.

By the many lines on the Mount of Luna, a Romany can see whatever creative talents a subject may have. If imagination is not balanced with intellect on the hand, it will suggest an unbalanced mind.

This mount covers a large area, and depending on the exact position of the apex, the nature of the person's imagination, creativity and emotion can be seen.

Many fine lines on the Mount of Luna show nervous tension; a small cross, superstition; a large cross, wild imagination; and a triangle, great talents and success.

Neptune　The lines or rascettes at the wrist are associated with this planet. They are a sign of material luck, and the number of lines on the wrist indicate the amount of such luck, although these lines are apt to change during life. One line means average luck; two, good luck; and three, wonderful luck.

FINGERS

Each finger is associated with the same planet as the mount at the base of it, and can modify or increase the qualities of each mount. Long fingers intensify, and short fingers decrease the qualities.

In addition, fingers which are long in relation to the length of the palm indicate idealism and interest in detail. If the first finger is unusually long it denotes a desire to rule; an over-long second finger, determination in religious matters; third finger, a gambling nature; and fourth finger, preoccupation with money.

Short fingers show a tendency to be materialistic and impetuous. Very short fingers suggest laziness and self-indulgence; slender fingers show delicacy; and coarse fingers, strong sensuality.

As you can see, no one aspect of a hand's size and shape is taken as a stated fact. It must always be related to the evidence of the hand as a whole. One aspect is frequently modified by another, and seeming contradictions, when studied by an expert Romany palmist, simply show the subtleties of human nature.

MAJOR LINES OF THE PALM

To describe the significance of *every* line on the palm would fill a whole book in itself. Here then are the meanings of just the basic lines.

The Life Line This starts above the thumb, encircles the Mount of Venus and often reaches as far as the wrist.

Firstly, and *most* important, the length of the Life Line does *not* indicate the length of life. Assessing that is a most complex study. Temporary illnesses are shown though in the form of a break, but if the Life Line is clear and well marked, and particularly if the break is not shown on the other hand, good health and energy will prevail in the life as a whole.

Lines rising from the Life Line are a sign of health and strength. If there is a longer line rising to the Mount of Jupiter it shows success. A connecting line to Saturn means a desire for solitude, and often indicates a deeply religious nature. A line to Uranus, providing it is straight, shows wealth or fame through the aids of family or friends. A thick unbroken line to Mercury means prosperity in business. A line to Upper Mars indicates bravery and physical strength.

Small lines descending towards the thumb show a need for love and affection, and small lines crossing the Life Line are known as bad luck lines. This type of bad luck is not of great consequence, and usually amounts to annoying interferences which cause temporary unhappiness.

A Line of Life which is forked at the end is a sign of an active and vigorous old age, and if there is a second line running parallel, that is a sign of another person's beneficial influence.

The Head Line   If the Life Line is attached at the top to the Line of Head for any but the smallest distance it indicates early dependence on parents. (Romanies, who can measure all lines quite precisely, can tell at what age each indication applies.) It also suggests a timid, shy childhood. Where Life and Head Lines are slightly separated it is a sign of an independent, adventurous and energetic nature. Wide separation means impulsiveness. When the lines just touch at the beginning it shows a moderately cautious and far-sighted person.

If the Line of Head slopes downwards towards Luna it shows a creative person with imagination and sensitivity. A straight horizontal Head Line extending to the edge of the palm suggests a person with an exceptionally good intellect, but self-centred and very demanding of others. Usually, the longer the line, the more intelligence.

A double Head Line means a surprise inheritance. A branch rising to Jupiter indicates wealth; to Uranus, interest in the arts; to Mercury, ability to help others. If there are small lines joining Head and Life Lines at the beginnings, this shows that the person is forced into earning a living contrary to ambition.

The Heart Line   This is the uppermost horizontal line, and runs from beneath the first or second finger to the outer edge of the palm.

Starting beneath the first finger, it is a sign of luck and

happiness in marriage. If it is too close to the finger though, it shows jealousy, and if too low, and running straight across the palm, it shows undemonstrative affection.

When the line starts between the first and second fingers, this is a sign of unselfish love. Starting under the third finger shows an unsympathetic attitude towards the opposite sex. If it should begin between the second and third fingers there will be a complete lack of understanding in love.

If the Heart Line runs parallel to the Head Line, it is a sign that the heart is ruled by the head. This is even more the case when the Heart Line descends to meet the Head Line. Where the Line of Head slopes downwards, away from the Line of Heart, it shows the opposite case of the head ruling the heart.

A double Heart Line indicates great capacity for love and affection.

Tiny lines which rise from the Line of Heart show happiness in love affairs, and descending ones show the disappointments.

When a Romany reads a hand he looks for a letter M for marriage formed on the palm. The first two strokes of the M are formed by the Life and Head Lines. The third stroke of the letter joins up the Heart Line with either the Line of Fortune or the Fate Line. It may be crudely formed, but the Gypsy can tell a late marriage (if the connecting line between Head and Heart Lines is low down) or if there are two marriages (two connecting lines).

Lines of Affection　Marriage is shown elsewhere in the hand, although serious love affairs will also be indicated here, in the Lines of Affection. They are horizontal lines on the very edge of the Mount of Mercury.

The longest, clearest line will be the most enduring relationship, and the order, timewise, is from the bottom up.

If a line slopes upward it shows no marriage, or a disappointing love affair. A broken line means separation or divorce, but if it breaks then continues overlapped, there will be a reconciliation.

Absence of a line may not necessarily mean no marriage, but that the marriage does not change the person's life-style.

The small lines crossing the Lines of Affection indicate children – straight lines for boys, slanting lines for girls.

Fate Line (or Line of Saturn)   This cannot be seen clearly on every hand, though its absence is not a bad sign. It indicates that the owner is more in command of his own destiny and not much influenced by Fate. Also, it may only appear on the palm in later years.

Often on a palm with a short Life Line, the life's pattern is shown on the Fate Line.

It runs straight up the centre of the palm, most commonly starting beside the Life Line and ending on the Mount of Saturn.

If the Fate Line is joined to the Life Line this is a fortunate sign, showing success in the chosen way of life. If it starts from the Mount of Venus, this shows early help in some form from the family. Starting from the 'rascettes', or wrist lines, means there are early difficulties to overcome. When the Fate Line begins on the Mount of Luna it indicates help given outside the family, and in addition it adds the intuitive and imaginative qualities of Luna to the career or way of life. Starting anywhere in the middle of the hand indicates a career started later in life. A change in careers is generally shown by a break in the Fate Line where it crosses the Line of Head, continuing from a different place.

If the Fate Line ends on the Mount of Jupiter it shows a good marriage or partnership. Ending on Saturn is a sign of Fate being kind throughout life. When it ends beneath the ring finger it indicates an artistic career.

The small lines cutting across the Fate Line are set-backs or obstacles, and an island formed on the line is financial loss.

Line of Fortune This also does not appear on every hand, or sometimes only a part of it is shown. Again, absence is not a bad omen, only an indication that personal effort will achieve success rather than 'luck'.

The Line of Fortune runs parallel to the Line of Fate, ending on the Mount of Uranus.

Where a Line of Fate is missing, the Line of Fortune may be read instead. If a palm has both clearly shown, this is a very good sign, showing that both success and fortune will rule the life.

The person with a clear, well-marked Line of Fortune will have the type of happy personality which attracts others, and leads to popularity. Such a disposition will mark him out as one of the 'lucky people' to whom wealth often comes easily. Fame, too, if the line ends in a star. If the ending is forked it signifies more than one talent. When the line is a broken one it shows different periods of success due to changes of life-style, marriage, ill-health, different interests or careers, etc.

The Line of Health (or Mercury)   There are very many ways in which a Romany can gauge health in a hand. One of the best indicators is the Line of Mercury – usually called the Health Line. It slants from the Mount of Mercury down towards the wrist.

Absence of this line is a good omen. It shows a strong constitution and only rare illness. Good health is also indicated if the line is straight and clear.

Any breaks in the line show periods of ill health. If the line is wavy, and especially if it starts on the Life Line, it shows a tendency to digestive troubles. When there is a branch pointing in the direction of the Mount of Jupiter, it means that health will cause a change in the way of life.

Other clues to the state of health a Romany can get from the colour of the hand. A red hand is a sign of an excitable, quick-tempered person who may suffer from high blood-pressure in later life. A pink palm with clearly marked lines is the sign of a fit, healthy person. Whilst a very pale palm with a lot of broken lines is a warning to be sensible in all aspects of health.

Rascettes, or wrist lines, which arch towards the palm are a sign that a careless attitude towards health must be avoided. It means that the person is inclined to take risks where health matters are concerned.

Where there is a triangle formed by the Lines of Health, Fate, and Life, this indicates a certain amount of second-sight. A person with this triangle should learn to trust his premonitions.

The Mystic Cross is occasionally found in the area between the Heart Line and the Head Line. This shows an interest in the mystical and the occult.

There are, of course, many more lines which are significant in palmistry. Indeed, there is an interpretation for every line on every palm.

If you look at your own hand or the hands of friends, you will very likely come across marks and lines that seem contradictory. You must remember that it takes a skilled palmist to interpret these signs correctly. When two lines seem to contradict each other, there may be another mark explaining why.

It must also be remembered – and this is the most important fact in any realm of fortune-telling – that all a palm, a pack of cards, or a horoscope can tell you about the future, are *trends* and *tendencies*, *opportunities* and *inclinations*. The exact future in store for you depends on what you make of these trends and opportunities. But since to be forewarned is to be forearmed, it may be a good idea to cross the Gypsy's palm with silver, and make sure you take all the right opportunities in life – and avoid the pitfalls!

NINE

Fortune-telling with Cards

Perhaps more than for anything else, the Romanies are famous for their skill at fortune-telling with cards. This is not really surprising since it was almost certainly the Gypsies who introduced the original playing cards to Europe in the early days of their migration. There is some controversy as to where exactly they brought them from. Some say from India, some from Persia, and, because the Gypsies called themselves 'Egyptians' many people claim they brought the cards from Egypt. The truth is lost in the mists of time.

The earliest Gypsy cards, called 'the Tarot', are the ancestors of the modern pack of playing cards. The Tarot is a beautiful and mysterious pack of cards, and has been used for fortune-telling for many centuries by occultists. It consists of seventy-eight cards (unlike the modern pack, which has just fifty-two cards and two jokers). Fifty-six of these are suit cards, called the 'Minor Arcana' and twenty-two are symbolically illustrated cards called the 'Major Arcana'.

The suit cards (Minor Arcana) are divided into Cups, Swords, Pentacles and Wands. In each suit there is a King,

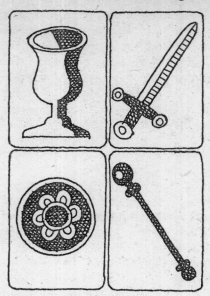

Queen, Knight, Page, and numbers from one, or ace, up to ten.

The Major Arcana cards consist of:

1. The Magician	12. The Hanged Man
2. The High Priestess	13. Death
3. The Empress	14. Temperance
4. The Emperor	15. The Devil
5. The Pope	16. The Falling Tower
6. The Lovers	17. The Star
7. The Chariot	18. The Moon
8. Justice	19. The Sun
9. The Hermit	20. The Last Judgement
10. The Wheel of Fortune	21. The World
11. Strength	0. The Fool

Each of the seventy-eight cards has significance, both for

the student of the occult, and for the wise old Romany fortune-teller, who has inherited her knowledge from her forbears, who in turn were given full interpretations hundreds of years ago from the wise men of the East.

The present-day pack has been considerably simplified to be suitable for the card games which it is mostly used for. The four Knights have been dropped from the Minor Arcana, leaving fifty-two suit cards. The Cups have become Hearts, the Swords, Spades, Pentacles are now Diamonds, and Wands are Clubs. The Major Arcana has been completely dropped, but for the curious survival of one card – the Fool, or Joker.

With this pack, a Gypsy woman can successfully predict, though perhaps in less depth than with a proper Tarot pack. Let us now see how she uses an ordinary, everyday pack of cards to tell fortunes.

Firstly, of course, each card has its own traditional meaning, as follows:

HEARTS

Hearts generally convey warmth and happiness, but also sensitivity and therefore possible pain and sorrow.

King A fair-haired man of influence and aristocratic bearing. Mature, intelligent, generous and likeable, but unreliable as an adviser as he is quick-tempered and hasty in judgement.

Queen A fair-haired, faithful, loving woman. Ideal wife,

mother, or lover. She may signify a potential rival in a woman's fortune, but one that is never mean or underhanded.

Jack   A close, long-standing friend, not necessarily a man. Not always to be trusted as he or she may gossip.

Ace   Home, and domestic life. Usually signifies love and joy, but can mean problems in the home.

Two   The success card. Means good luck, achievement of goals.

Three   Impetuous action, unwise choice or indecision.

Four   Long-delayed marriage or celibacy. Anxiety.

Five   Indecision. Difficulties in making a choice. Can indicate change of surroundings.

Six   This shows a weakness, either in body or character. An overgenerous nature may be taken advantage of. Can even indicate intrigue.

Seven   Disappointments. Don't depend on other people as they are likely to break promises made.

Eight   A happy occasion. A party, or gay company.

Nine   The 'wish card'. Dreams come true. Success and harmony.

Ten   A lucky card. A surprise in the form of success or good fortune. Could be news of a marriage.

SPADES

These are the warning cards. They indicate bad luck, interference and losses, but if heed is taken through these cards, misfortune can be averted.

King   A tall, dark man. Ambitious and potentially dangerous in business or in love.

Queen   Sign of a fascinating but cruel, treacherous woman.

Jack   An untrustworthy friend. A younger person who is lazy and will exploit and hinder.

Ace   The death card. *Not to be taken literally though* as it usually refers to bad news of any type and especially to broken relationships or emotional conflicts with dear ones.

Two   Complete change or separation. Change of home; journey abroad. Separation from friends or loved ones.

Three   An unhappy card signifying misfortune and often failure in love or marriage.

Four   Temporary misfortune. A minor illness or financial upset. Guard against jealousy.

Five   This card indicates that success in career or marriage will be attained, but only after many setbacks. Optimism can be maintained.

Six Good luck will come in time. Perseverance, hard work and careful foresight will eventually be rewarded. Don't be easily discouraged.

Seven Quarrels and tears. To avoid suffering, keep your peace with friends and relatives until this difficult period passes.

Eight Card of opposition. Check at once any legal matters on hand, or trusted friends. Treachery can be avoided if this advice is followed.

Nine The unluckiest card of all. Can mean misery, loss of money or great misfortune. Can only be avoided by making sure you maintain the highest intentions.

Ten Another bad card, this cancels out the good signs of accompanying cards. If accompanying cards are bad, this one strengthens their influence.

DIAMONDS

As you might expect, the cards of the Diamond suit stand for money. Also the practical, lowly side of life. They signify legal, political, financial and family matters.

King A dangerous man with strong features and cold blue eyes. A ruthless competitor in business, he is feared by other men. For a woman, he could mean a deceitful or hard-hearted husband or lover, and could only be made affectionate and reasonable by a very understanding woman.

Queen   Pretty and flirtatious woman. Attractive only to men. Given to gossip and interference. Her character could be enhanced only by the influence of a tender but firm man.

Jack   A messenger – usually a man. Seldom harmful towards another man, but a danger to women. Selfish and deceitful.

Ace   An important message. It could be a letter, a gift, money, or an engagement ring.

Two   A great love affair will loom more important than anything else.

Three   Disagreement. Disputes in business and in the home. Sign of separation or divorce.

Four   Quarrels with friends or family. Shows a neglected friendship or frequent quarrels with the family. Interference from relatives.

Five   Prosperity either in career or marriage. Honest business transactions bring long-standing friendship. In marriage, prosperity, happiness and a pride in children.

Six   An early marriage may be a failure. If a second marriage is being considered, it is a sign that caution is required or that also may be unhappy.

Seven   Unlucky card, especially for a gambler. False rumours and unkind words hurt.

Eight   This card indicates a rural life. It can also show a marriage or a journey late in life – perhaps both.

Nine   An adventure card. Could mean an exciting journey, or some unexpected financial news.

Ten This card concerns money. It might mean a journey in connection with money, or a surprise marriage with money involved.

CLUBS

These cards are connected with activity, energy and enterprise. They indicate friendship and the importance of influence.

King A strong, dark man. A valuable and stalwart friend. Loyal, honest and sincere.

Queen A dark, beautiful woman. A trustworthy, affectionate friend and a loyal and loving wife. Sometimes temperamental.

Jack Not always a man, this card indicates a sincere friend. Generous and cheerful. Capable of well-intentioned flattery.

Ace The sign of many good friends. Also an indication of financial success, and even fame, in career.

Two Friends are against you in some matter. Do not look for support, but go it alone.

Three A long association resulting in marriage. Sometimes indicates re-marriage.

Four A danger card. Indicates a sudden misfortune, disappointing outcome of a venture; accident. Beware of friends who are not all they seem.

Five   If care is taken – a prosperous marriage.

Six   A sign of successful business based on friendship with partners, employers, or employees.

Seven   Good luck will come your way provided you avoid interference from the opposite sex.

Eight   Do not be tempted to borrow by your need for money. It will lead to broken friendships.

Nine   Avoid quarrels – they will cause a lot of trouble for you. Goals will be attained by a broad-minded, flexible approach.

Ten   A powerful good luck card which brings unexpected happiness in some form. Either an inheritance, a successful journey, a misfortune averted, or reunion with a long lost friend.

Each card has its traditional significance, but must always be read in the context of the other cards close by. This is, of course, where the Romany uses her intuitive skill.

Unlike palmistry or astrology, a session with a Gypsy reading the cards is carried out with the assistance of the person whose fortune is being read. The Gypsy will ask questions of the *gorgio*, and his answers will help her to understand the cards correctly. The cards will reveal information and advice, rather than a straight revelation of past, present and future. Helpful cooperation then, is necessary in order to get a really useful reading.

The Romanies use several different methods of actually laying out the cards. If the 'client' wants to learn more on a particular point, the fortune-teller may lay out the cards again in a different manner and thereby get a new slant on the problem.

However the cards are to be laid out, the Gypsy first asks

the client to shuffle the pack. If the cards need to be cut, the client must do this with his left hand (or his right if he is left-handed).

Some methods require that a single card called a 'Significator' be chosen. This is the card which most represents the client. It can be the Joker, which doesn't literally mean the 'Fool' of the Tarot, but rather, the everyman, the uninitiated. Alternatively, it could be one of the court cards. A King for a man, a Queen for a woman, and for a young woman or youth, a Jack. A person with dark hair and eyes would be represented by a court card from the Spades suit. Fair hair and blue eyes from the Clubs, light brown or fair hair with dark eyes from Diamonds, and dark hair and blue, grey or hazel eyes from the Hearts.

Here are some of the simpler methods used:

THE MYSTIC CROSS

This is a quick method which is useful if the client has one special question on his mind.

To begin with, the Significator is decided upon; the Jokers are removed from the pack; and then the client shuffles the cards.

The Gypsy lays them out in the form of a cross working top to bottom, then left to right. Each arm consists of three

cards. Vertical and horizontal axes are made up of seven cards each. There are thirteen cards on the table. Three, seven and thirteen are the most mystical numbers of all.

The Gypsy then turns over the cards, one at a time, starting with the vertical row from top to bottom, which states the client's existing situation, then the three cards on the left which influence the fortune for good or bad, and finally the three on the right which tell the outcome.

If the Significator is amongst the thirteen, that is a very good sign.

THE MYSTIC STAR

In this method the client's Significator is first placed in the centre of the table, then the client shuffles the cards. Next the Gypsy lays out the cards in the following numbered

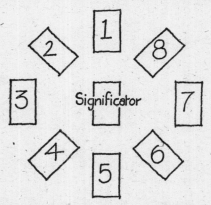

sequence, placing them face downwards and in anti-clockwise order.

She then hands the remainder of the pack to the client and asks him to place two additional cards face downwards on each point of the star, in the same order.

Still working in an anti-clockwise direction and in the

same sequence, the Gypsy turns over the groups of three cards, one group at a time, reading what she sees there. Finally she will make a complete summary of the reading.

THE WHEEL OF FORTUNE

Again, the Significator is placed in the centre and the client shuffles the cards. Then the Gypsy places nine piles of three cards each in the following numerical order, placing the remaining cards in a pile at the right-hand side.

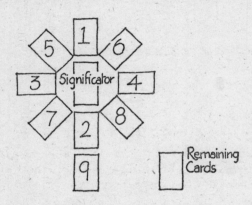

She then reads them, drawing three cards at a time from the remainder pile, if any point needs to be clarified.

LUCKY THIRTEEN

As usual the Significator goes in the centre and the client shuffles the pack. Then the Gypsy lays out thirteen cards in the following pattern and alphabetical order A–A; B–B; C–C, and so on. She then reads them in pairs.

Pair A represent the client; pair B the client's closest influences; pairs C and D indicate the future; and pairs E and F are secondary influences to the client.

This method may be used three times, in which case the first lay-out will signify the past; the second, the present; and the third, the future.

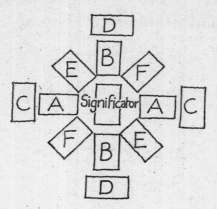

THE SEVEN TRIPLETS

After shuffling, the client cuts the pack into three piles. The Gypsy takes one card from each pile and places them face upwards in seven separate groups of three, like this:

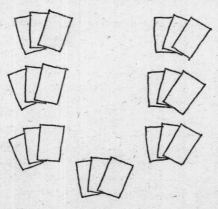

In each group it will be the middle card (which will have come from the middle heap) about which the prediction is concerned. The other two flanking cards will relate to it.

As with palmistry, fortune-telling by cards tries to indicate to the client the *possibilities*, *trends* and *opportunities* of his life, rather than any definite certainties. (In this life nothing is definite; man is, or should be, ultimate master of his own destiny.)

TEN

Gypsies and Astrology

Astrology is known as the oldest science, but for centuries it had a bad reputation because of a minority of non-gypsy astrologers who used the knowledge they gained for their own evil ends. People feared this skill which they couldn't understand, and believed all astrologers to be in league with the devil. Then, in later years, with so many visible signs of scientific progress, people tended to dismiss the whole subject as simply superstitious nonsense.

It is only in the last few years that even the most down-to-earth scientists are beginning to accept the idea that perhaps heavenly bodies transmit rays which affect us on this earth. They are beginning to get scientific proof that the position of the planets in the sky affects more than just the tides. The magnetic pull of the full moon, for instance, has a definite influence on people suffering from mental illness. There is modern proof of this old wives' tale: if the moon can influence such things as men's minds, and the tides on this planet, it is not so incredible that the position of all the other planets in the sky should have influence on us through the transmission of rays.

And while fashionable ideas of the western world come and go, the Romany practises with calm certainty the beliefs inherited from his ancestors of the eastern world hundreds of years ago. Whilst learned scientists debate the possibility of planetary influences, the Romany sincerely believes that if he constructs a horoscope, he can acquire knowledge of a person or events.

Few people believe that the whole of mankind is divided into just twelve categories, as the horoscopes in newspapers and magazines would lead us to suppose. In fact these readings are only very broad guides, and are intended to be read as such. A true Gypsy horoscope takes into account the position of *every* planet at the time of your birth, not just the sun, so you will see that this is a far more complex thing.

For a full horoscope then, the Romany will need to know from you the date of your birth, the exact time you were born, and the place. With this information he can work out quite precisely, with the help of complicated tables, the position in the sky of every planet at the moment of your birth as seen from the place of your birth. The position of each planet is believed to influence your life and character in a very definite way. You will realize, that as with palmistry, no two people will have quite the same horoscope. Even twins are not born simultaneously, although, as with other people born on the same day, their general character and life-pattern will be broadly similar.

As you may know, there are twelve signs in the Zodiac, and each sign covers roughly, a month of the year. The sign gets its name and symbol from a particular constellation or group of stars in the sky.

Time	Sign	Symbol	Glyph or Mark
21 March – 20 April	Aries	Ram	♈
21 April – 20 May	Taurus	Bull	♉

21 May – 20 June	Gemini	Twins	♊
21 June – 21 July	Cancer	Crab	♋
22 July – 21 Aug	Leo	Lion	♌
22 Aug – 21 Sept	Virgo	Virgin	♍
22 Sept – 22 Oct	Libra	Scales	♎
23 Oct – 21 Nov	Scorpio	Scorpion	♏
22 Nov – 20 Dec	Sagittarius	Archer	♐
21 Dec – 19 Jan	Capricorn	Goat	♑
20 Jan – 18 Feb	Aquarius	Water Bearer	♒
19 Feb – 20 March	Pisces	Fishes	♓

Each sign is ruled by a planet which also has a traditional glyph or mark:

Planet	*Glyph*	*Governs*
Sun	☉	Leo
Moon	☽	Cancer
Mercury	☿	Gemini and Virgo

Venus		Taurus and Libra
Mars		Aries and Scorpio
Jupiter		Sagittarius and Pisces
Saturn		Capricorn and Aquarius
Uranus		Aquarius (together with Saturn)
Neptune		Pisces (together with Jupiter)
Pluto		Scorpio (together with Mars)

A horoscope is in fact a *map*, or *chart*, of the solar system at a given moment in time. First of all a circle is drawn to represent the heavens, with a smaller circle in the centre to represent the earth. The heavens are then divided into twelve imaginary sections or houses. With the help of highly complex tables the Gypsy astrologer can work out the position of each sign in relation to each house, and also the position of all the planets.

Each house is concerned with a particular aspect of your life:

1st House: Personal appearance, both physical and personality as shown to others.

2nd House: Material possessions and money.

3rd House: Intellect. Communication. Short journeys.

4th House: Domesticity. Relationship with mother.

5th House: Love life. Children. Creativity. Pleasures and amusements.

6th House: Work. Health. Service to and from others.

7th House: One's opposite number in marriage, business, etc.

8th House: Any death which personally affects one. Inheritances, either material or characteristics.

9th House: Religion and philosophy. Foreign travel.

10th House: Career. Reputation. Relationship with father.

11th House: Social position, friendships.
12th House: Inner life. Seclusion. Secrets.

Once the Romany has drawn up such a chart, his knowledge and intuition enable him to interpret the horoscope with great accuracy.

As you can see, the drawing-up of a complete horoscope is a complicated task which only an astrologer can do. But simply knowing a person's Sun sign, which is the sign through which the Sun was moving at the time of birth, can be interesting on its own.

First we must know that each sign is also ruled by one of the elements: Fire, Earth, Air or Water as follows:

Fire   { Aries
          Leo
          Sagittarius

Earth   { Taurus
          Virgo
          Capricorn

Air   { Gemini
          Libra
          Aquarius

Water   { Cancer
          Scorpio
          Pisces

Briefly, the Fire signs are characterized by inspiration, Earth by practicality, Air by intellect, and Water by emotion. Here is a short description of the supposed characteristics of people born under the twelve signs. Find out the birth dates of your friends and see if they fit their astrological descriptions.

ARIES (21 March – 20 April)

The Arian is ambitious and self-assertive. He is intellectually very capable, and physically active and energetic. He loves to fight for a good cause and thrives on praise, but cannot tolerate interference or restriction. Self-reliant, idealistic, very courageous and enthusiastic, he is an ideal person to initiate and take command of any scheme.

He must be careful not to antagonize his family and colleagues by being tactless and wilful. He must remember to listen, and consider the other point of view. He has an aggressive temper which is quickly roused, but just as quickly subsides. He should learn to develop self-restraint and consideration for the feelings of others.

TAURUS (21 April – 20 May)

People born when the Sun is in Taurus will be the practical, reliable, steady, plodding type. The person who will always win his goal by dogged, unswerving perseverance. His methods may seem old-fashioned and conservative to people in more volatile signs, and being strong-willed, he can be irritatingly unadaptable and fixed in his ways. However, he is generous, reliable, faithful, kind-hearted, gentle and full of feeling for others. He is slow to anger, but once aroused can show, like the bull, an uncontrollable temper. Also like the bull he can be led but not driven.

His ruler is Venus which makes him romantic, affectionate, artistic and sensual. He appreciates all the good things of life – the comforts and all beautiful things. For this reason he tends to be materialistic, collecting around himself possessions, not so much for their monetary value as for the pleasure and comfort they afford him. He must be careful to keep these pleasures of the senses within reasonable bounds or he may become over-indulgent. He must also beware of obstinacy, conceit, slovenliness, and his greatest enemy, laziness.

Of the arts, the Taurean is more inclined to that of music and often has a good singing voice.

GEMINI (21 May – 20 June)

The Gemini subject is ruled by Mercury. He is full of restless energy. He is intelligent and his lively mind is always ready for fresh knowledge. He is quick in physical movement, speech and intellect. He thrives on change and can quickly adapt himself to new circumstances. He finds travel stimulating, and the company of others indispensable, although preferring people of superior, or at least equal, intelligence. The Geminian is a great talker and with his sparkle, his great imagination and wit, is gay company. In addition to his quickly perceptive brain, he is usually clever with his hands.

One of the greatest dangers for a Geminian is that his many interests may prevent him examining any one thing to sufficient depth. Often this flitting from subject to subject produces a shallow nature. He is frequently accused of being over-talkative, irresponsible, superficial, and neglectful of former friendships.

He is of a nervous disposition and the Twins being a double-bodied sign, you may not always know where you are with a Geminian. He can alternate his gaiety with black moods of despair, although they will not last long.

CANCER (21 June – 21 July)

This is a sign governed by the element Water and is ruled by the Moon. People born under this sign are very sensitive, emotional, imaginative and proud. They have receptive minds, and are often very intelligent.

Like the crab, the Cancerian is very tenacious, and this tenacity shows itself in many ways. Once a scheme, idea or project has won his heart, he will take a grip on it until he has carried it through to the end, which behaviour, though commendable, may make him appear stubborn to others. He clings to memories, so that he can recall in detail events which took place years before. He is often prejudiced, since he will cling to his own personal set of views or values, which colours all new ideas presented to him and limits his vision. Finally, he clings to what is his. His family and the security of his home mean a lot to him. He appreciates home comforts and luxuries, and is often fond of antiques, old customs and traditions.

The Cancerian woman makes a good mother and takes a great pride in her family. Woe betide anyone who criticizes her husband or children, for her sensitive nature is quickly wounded and she can be quite vindictive once she gets her claws into someone. She must guard against over-possessiveness with her family.

As we saw in palmistry, the influence of the Moon makes for an artistic nature, and many Cancerians are artists of one kind of another. Their sensitive imagination is well-channelled into music, painting, writing, etc.

LEO (22 July – 21 August)

The Leo individual is a born leader of men. Masterful and fearless, like the lion, he likes to lord it. He has great pride and an enormous amount of willpower. He is ambitious and has the ability of long-sustained effort.

Leo is a fire sign and ruled by the Sun. As may be imagined, this gives him great warmth of personality and he is a loyal and faithful friend, cheerful, sociable, warm-hearted and generous – though he does like to be respected for his qualities!

He is open-hearted, trustworthy, and makes a point of

being scrupulously honest, though sometimes lack of tact can earn him enemies.

Providing his aims in life are worthwhile, his inner strength, honesty, authoritative manner and sunny disposition will ensure success. He must be prepared, however, to learn leniency, for his convictions formed early in life are seldom changed and this can make for narrow-mindedness and impatience with others. He should also be careful to avoid becoming arrogant and egotistical.

He cares much for outward appearances and when his pride is offended, he will fly into a temper and say things he will regret later. His rage is short-lived, however, and he is quick to forgive. If he sees himself to have been in the wrong, he will be the first to apologize.

It is a curious fact that left-handed people invariably have Leo strongly aspected in their horoscope, though not always as their sun sign.

VIRGO (22 August – 21 September)

The Virgoan is intelligent, logical, practical and shrewd. He has an analytical mind, is clear-thinking and methodical, and a great perfectionist. He sets high moral standards both for himself and others, and can therefore be very critical.

He is fond of detail and usually very tidy and methodical in his habits; very health-conscious, and considers his diet carefully.

Although modest and reserved, the Virgoan is very friendly and indeed a very good friend to have. Infinitely kind-hearted and sympathetic, he excels at helping others with his usual shrewdness, and practical, down-to-earth approach. He is generous, unselfish, diplomatic, conscientious and hard-working. He is not inclined to lose his temper, but can fret and fuss over minor irritations, and seethe inwardly over bigger upsets.

The Virgoan sometimes suffers a lack of self-confidence, and occasionally the highly moral aspect of his nature can be reversed, producing the most unscrupulous rogue.

LIBRA (22 September – 22 October)

The sign of the Scales represents balance and the Libran strives for just that in all aspects of his life. He values harmony and order in everything.

He will avoid extremist views, and does not get along well with people of fixed ideas as he instinctively likes to consider every side of a situation before giving his judgement – which will probably be an impartial one.

This admirable quality of seeking fair judgement can have two disadvantages in *some* Librans. One being difficulty in making a decision or taking a line of action, as their anxiety to be scrupulously fair will sometimes make them reluctant to make a final choice. They can be evasive and indecisive. The other disadvantage is an uncontrollable habit of comparing and criticizing all he sees. These people have a compulsion to be for ever drawing conclusions, which can be most annoying for those around them. They are so inquisitive that they will frequently air their opinions in circumstances which are none of their business. These Librans must learn to keep their own council, or their critical nature will destroy their chances of happiness.

Most Librans, however, are so fond of harmonious relationships that they will avoid unpleasant scenes or disagreement with others.

They are perceptive and intuitive, and appreciate beauty and luxury in their surroundings. They have good taste and are usually elegant and attractive to look at. The women are mostly pretty and engaging with essentially feminine ways. The men have charming manners. Librans are tactful, friendly, courteous and popular. They have a refined artistic sense, and there are many artists amongst them.

If they can develop perseverance and sufficient willpower, their open-minded approach and sense of what is right will see them well through life. They thrive best in beautiful and peaceful surroundings.

SCORPIO (23 October – 21 November)

The Scorpio subject is very strong-willed, courageous, self-confident and direct in manner. He has a magnetic and sometimes even hypnotic attraction for others.

His greatest feature is the ability to penetrate and know the quality of any situation or problem. Scorpions make excellent doctors, surgeons, healers, detectives and research workers. This gift also enables them to be extraordinarily perceptive where other people are concerned. They can quickly detect any flaw in another's character, but must be careful to put this insight to good use and not dwell on the bad to the exclusion of the good.

The Scorpion may be able to read other people like a book, but his own book remains strictly closed, for he delights in secrecy and mystery and often appears over-reserved. He has a dignified, inscrutable air of calmness and quiet watchfulness.

Some Scorpions, unknown to themselves, have the spiritual power of healing and should try to develop this. Scorpio also needs to develop tact, and check a tendency towards sarcasm.

The Scorpio subject is sensitive, for all his strength of character, and the best way to influence him is to appeal to his emotions.

He is a passionate lover and tends to be jealous, showing a quite vicious temper when roused. He knows how to use the sting in the Scorpion's tail when cornered, and when seriously provoked can be relentless in his attack.

SAGITTARIUS (22 November – 20 December)

The Sagittarian is idealistic and a true lover of freedom. He is usually a popular person, happy-go-lucky, tolerant and sociable, with a keen sense of humour and a kind heart. He can sometimes be recognized by his expressive eyes which are open, frank and kindly. There is also sometimes an irregularity of the front teeth.

His extrovert nature feels the need for companionship, and he is happiest when he has someone to talk to. He is certainly a great talker – although a good listener, too. He loves to discuss his ideas, and is ready to be brought round to another's point of view providing a good enough argument is put forward. He is honest, and can be confidently trusted with the most personal secrets.

Sagittarians are optimists, even through the most difficult times. They are very energetic and fond of change and travel. They make first-class linguists, and they are invariably animal-lovers.

Like all the Fire signs, the Sagittarian has a temper when roused, and his keen intuition tells him how best to wound his opponent. His anger is quickest aroused by some wrong done either to himself or another, for he has a great sense of justice and is both morally and physically quite fearless.

Although a Sagittarian likes variety and change, he is well-advised to choose one career wisely and stick to it. For his considerable willpower is best directed at one goal, and not dissipated on many other, less worthwhile activities. He should learn the value of tact as such forthright people can so easily give offence to the more sensitive. It might also pay him on occasion to be less frank about some of his ambitions!

Other faults are likely to be restlessness, lack of concentration, irritability, extravagance and carelessness. They are often so preoccupied with their ultimate goal that they neglect to attend to the ordinary everyday matters.

CAPRICORN (21 December – 19 January)

The Capricorn subject is very ambitious, and he invariably achieves his ambitions because of his industrious, practical, cautious and steadfast nature. The male Capricornian is the world's most successful in whatever career he takes up. The Capricornian woman, besides making a good business-woman is a dutiful, thrifty and prudent wife and mother, who is full of ambition for her family.

They are logical in their approach, diplomatic and tactful, quiet, earnest, reliable and contemplative. They are con-servative, and dislike the unconventional or unorthodox. They have their own very definite views, and dislike the suggestion that they may be wrong. They are generally tidy, and always methodical in their habits.

The Capricornian is a materialist at heart. He is curiously limited by a sense of predestination and fate. This sometimes causes him to miss chances which come his way, and very often his life is a hard one. He invariably accepts his lot with good heart, however. His innate calm stability and industrious perseverance see him through, and strengthen his character into the bargain. The second half of his life is nearly always the happiest. Some Capricornians can be gloomily pessimistic, and even morose, but many possess a keen, though quiet wit.

The Capricornian is a forceful character with a constant desire to dominate. He is a great organizer and always does well in a position of authority, being conscientious and dutiful, qualities which he looks for in his employees.

He is always self-possessed, often self-centred, and he likes to be appreciated. Although he has a kind, affectionate nature, he often finds himself feared or respected rather than liked or loved. He is slow to forgive his enemies, and some Capricornians can be quite vindictive and malicious. Other faults in this sign of otherwise sterling qualities, are jealousy, suspicion, prejudice, a tendency to be domineering, and a craving for prestige and homage.

AQUARIUS (20 January – 18 February)

The Aquarian is by nature a scientist and a humanitarian.

He is attracted to all scientific subjects and is fascinated by anything new and original. New ideas, inventions, gadgets, theories, all delight his inquiring mind. He enjoys any sort of research, and new concepts of any kind must be tried and tested before he will accept them. Nothing is taken at face value.

He is likewise fascinated by all living things. Plant life interests him, he is a great animal-lover, and above all is his great concern for humanity. The Aquarian is quick to read and understand another's character, and he is always willing to aid those in need of help or advice.

Like the Scorpion, the Aquarian has a strangely magnetic personality. He has a friendly though undemonstrative disposition, and no sacrifice is too great for a friend. He can be disconcerting, however, for he feels the need from time to time, either to be alone, or to be very silent and withdrawn, often for no apparent reason, and can be difficult to get on with at these times.

The Aquarian is generally erratic and unpredictable in his behaviour. He can take offence at the most unexpected things which often earns him the reputation of being touchy. He is frequently eccentric in his ways, and is a difficult person to understand. Once an enemy is made it is for ever.

He is intellectual, idealistic, strong-willed and enterprising. He has a refined artistic taste, and is frequently gifted in literary subjects. He is an unconventional person who always has a stock of exciting, original ideas and opinions. He is stimulating, if somewhat mysterious, company.

PISCES (19 February – 20 March)

Pisces is the twelfth and last sign of the Zodiac, and because each successive sign takes many of the attributes of the foregoing signs, adding to these, more prominently, the particular attributes of its own sign, you will see that Pisces is the most complex of all, and Pisceans are difficult people to fully understand. They frequently give false impressions.

Their deep nature is a very emotional and sensitive one and they have a great capacity for quickly sensing the thoughts and feelings of others. They are sympathetic, easy-going, patient, generous and tactful. Always ready to help and support other people and frequently making sacrifices for the sake of others.

They do need encouragement and appreciation, however, and if their kindness is not acknowledged, or they are taken advantage of, they are quickly hurt and will retire into the background.

The Piscean is basically shy and appears quiet and dreamy. His thoughtfulness and reticence often causes him to be overlooked. Less sensitive people mistake his quietness for shallowness, not understanding that the subtle qualities of his nature are manifest inwardly and that he is at odds with the outward 'show' of society.

As may be expected with someone not always understood, the Piscean is inclined to feel despondent. Nevertheless, his ruling planet, Jupiter, ensures that his life is mostly lucky, and so long as he steers clear of most of the Piscean faults, he will find success – not in business so much as in some artistic or humane way where natural talent can be used. There are many Pisceans in show business, literary work, music, painting and dancing. And many more where service to others is required, such as nursing, secretarial work, catering and the armed forces.

The most common faults of the Piscean are lack of concentration, peevishness, deceit, lack of self-confidence and initiative. He is easily discouraged, sometimes unsociable, an escapist, or even an alcoholic. Unless his moral standards remain high, he is easy prey to the influence of bad company.

His extraordinary adaptability and knack of sympathetically sensing the feelings of another, make him unite himself with that person, often making it difficult to retain his own identity. He will then be accused of lacking will-power, of being weak, easily influenced, hypocritical and of being knocked from pillar to post. If he can learn to help and sympathize without becoming too identified with other people it will be much better for him.

As with all double-bodied signs, he often has difficulty in making up his mind on a course of action, and with Pisces, this is frequently because he doesn't want to hurt someone, and because he hates a scene.

The Piscean is friendly, hospitable, forgiving, and a true romantic. He is methodical by nature and likes law and order. He is always more influenced by emotion than by logic. Providing he has a strong sense of purpose he will make a success of his life.

Astrologers point out that many of the characteristics of a sign can, in some people, be reversed. Therefore, positive aspects can become negative, producing quite the opposite type. For instance, the usual tidiness and order of a Virgo subject, can occasionally be reversed to produce a very *un*tidy person, but in any event the very untidiness and disorder will be a 'thing' with them.

CUSPS

Of course, the earth revolves steadily, and we do not jump from the influence of one planet, or sign of the Zodiac, to the next. It is a gradual process, and it takes a few days for us to pass from the influence of one sign into another. These periods are called cusps, and people born two or three days either side of the line, i.e. with birthdays at the beginning or end of a sun sign, are known as cuspal subjects. They will have some characteristics of both signs.

Gypsy astrologers also believe they can work out which signs are likely to get along well with which. They think that a person will have easiest relationships with people ruled by the same *element* (Earth, Air, Fire, Water) as himself, so that all the Earth signs tend to understand each other, all the Water signs, and so on. Here is a list of the twelve sun signs which tells you which are the most compatible.

ARIES Sagittarius Leo Libra Gemini Aquarius

TAURUS Capricorn Virgo Scorpio Pisces Cancer

GEMINI Libra Aquarius Sagittarius Aries Leo

CANCER Scorpio Pisces Capricorn Virgo Taurus

LEO Aries Sagittarius Aquarius Gemini Libra

VIRGO Taurus Capricorn Pisces Scorpio Cancer

LIBRA Aquarius Gemini Aries Leo Sagittarius

SCORPIO Cancer Pisces Taurus Virgo Capricorn

SAGITTARIUS Leo Aries Gemini Libra Aquarius

CAPRICORN Taurus Virgo Cancer Scorpio Pisces

AQUARIUS Gemini Libra Leo Sagittarius Aries

PISCES Scorpio Cancer Virgo Taurus Capricorn

Of course these are generalities, and much depends on the individual horoscope.

Perhaps surprisingly, people with the *same* Sun signs rarely hit it off well together. Whilst they may have a considerable understanding of each other, they tend either to find each other intolerably boring and predictable, or else their evenly-matched characteristics cause the sparks to fly!

Finally, the Romany will know everything which will bring you luck. All these so-called 'lucky' things are based on the astrological influences, sympathetic to your sun sign or ruling planet.

Here are some of them:

ARIES

Number	1 and 9
Day	Tuesday
Colour	Crimson
Gem	Diamond or sapphire
Plants	Thistle, hawthorn, oak
Metal	Iron
Strongest Sense	Taste

TAURUS

Number	6
Day	Friday
Colour	Blue
Gem	Emerald or turquoise
Plants	Violet, primula, poppy, cherry tree
Metal	Copper
Strongest Sense	Touch

GEMINI

Number	5
Day	Wednesday
Colour	Yellow
Gem	Opal or agate
Plants	Lavender, clover, mulberry tree
Metal	Quicksilver
Strongest Sense	Eyesight

CANCER

Number	2 and 7
Day	Monday
Colour	Violet
Gem	Pearl and ruby
Plants	Lily, iris, narcissus, olive and willow trees
Metal	Silver
Strongest Sense	Cancer is ruled by the moon which seems to have no particular effect on any one of the senses.

LEO

Number	1 and 4
Day	Sunday
Colour	Orange
Gem	Sardonyx
Plants	Rose, sunflower, pimpernel
Metal	Gold
Strongest Sense	Leo is ruled by the sun which seems to have no particular effect on any one of the senses.

VIRGO

Number	5
Day	Wednesday
Colour	Yellow and blue
Gem	Crysolite
Plants	Lily-of-the-valley, myrtle, ash tree
Metal	Quicksilver
Strongest Sense	Eyesight

LIBRA

Number	6
Day	Friday
Colour	Blue and green
Gem	Opal
Plants	Lilac, alpine rose, mignonette, plum and pear trees
Metal	Copper
Strongest Sense	Touch

SCORPIO

Number	9
Day	Tuesday
Colour	Red
Gem	Topaz
Plants	Cactus, heather, boxwood
Metal	Iron
Strongest Sense	Taste

SAGITTARIUS

Number	3
Day	Thursday
Colour	Purple
Gem	Turquoise
Plants	Rose, cornflower, chestnut and fig trees
Metal	Tin
Strongest Sense	Smell

CAPRICORN

Number	8
Day	Saturday
Colour	Green
Gem	Garnet
Plants	Pansy, holly, ivy, quince and palm trees
Metal	Lead
Strongest Sense	Hearing

AQUARIUS

Number	8 and 4
Day	Saturday and Wednesday
Colour	Light green
Gem	Amethyst and amber
Plants	Daffodils, mistletoe, evergreens, beech, ash and poplar trees
Metal	Lead and platinum
Strongest Sense	Hearing and clairvoyance (psychic sight)

PISCES

Number	7
Day	Thursday and Friday
Colour	Silver and light grey
Gem	Bloodstone and aquamarine
Plants	Carnation, water lily, horse chestnut and apricot trees
Metal	Tin and aluminium
Strongest Sense	Smell and clairaudience (psychic hearing)

ELEVEN

Gypsies in the Future

This book has told you many of the Gypsies' secrets and much about their way of life. But what does the future hold for them?

Certainly they face a formidable challenge at the present time. In the old days it was easy for large groups of Romany wagons to travel the roads, stopping on heath and common-land. They found it fairly easy to lead their own independent lives. Nowadays, with such an increase in population and productivity, places where a caravan may stop without fear of harassment are becoming fewer and fewer. Land is too valuable ever to be called 'free'. Even the dwindling areas of common-land are being jealously guarded by increasing numbers of local ratepayers who want, not surprisingly, to keep green spaces clear.

Here then is the Gypsies' main problem. The law is against them at every turn: they are not allowed to camp on the roadside, so that they are faced with the impossible situation of travelling along roads on which they are literally forbidden to stop, and they therefore have no option but to break the law.

There are, however, some *gorgio* people who feel strongly for the *Rom*, and for several years they have been helping them to press for official recognition of their plight. They want it made possible for the Romanies to keep to their own way of life rather than be forced to adopt ours, as has been attempted in the past when local authorities have provided houses for Gypsies, making it necessary for them to get permanent jobs and send their children to *gorgio* schools. In fact where this happened practically none of the families stayed in these new homes. After a short while most were back on the road again.

In 1968 Parliament passed its first law ever in favour of Gypsies. It required that every County Council should provide a camping-site with proper facilities to accomodate all the *Rom* in the area in exchange for a fair rent. It also required all City Boroughs to provide a site for fifteen families. And this would seem to be the perfect answer to the problem, but unfortunately progress has been very slow, and many local authorities are objecting, either through prejudice, or through the lack of available land.

Up to the time of writing, sixty-two sites have been established out of the goal of 300 for England and Wales. Twenty of these are in London, though twelve London boroughs have yet to provide one.

When all objections have been overcome and there is a site in every area, preferably run by the Gypsies themselves as this has proved most successful, then the Romanies will be able to travel once more with freedom.

Another problem they have to face is education. Although the *Rom* have no desire for their children to be given a *gorgio* education, they naturally want them to be able to read and write in order to hold their own in today's world.

For the sake of the children's education a Romany family will sometimes stay in one place just long enough to enable the children to become literate, before resuming their travels.

But Gypsy children hate the *gorgio* schools. They are not used to the restrictions they meet there, and especially resent such 'grouping-off' of children from adults. They are accustomed to mixing freely with all ages and dislike school as much as an elderly Romany would hate an Old People's Home.

Also, once a Gypsy child reaches the age of about eleven, he or she is treated within the family as a small grown-up. The girls help to mind the younger children, or sell flowers in the street, whilst the boys help their father and uncles with such things as scrap-dealing. They certainly resent going to school at that age, and being treated as children.

The ideal answer to this problem would be eventually to have a small school at each camping-site to cater for the children on that site. There are in fact twelve schools at present operating especially for Britain's Gypsy children, though during August this number is increased to fifty so that quite a large number of children can be prepared for the normal schools they will attend in September. Most of these schools are travelling schools, and are converted buses or coaches which look just like classrooms inside. Some are parked on sites semi-permanently, and others actually travel around with groups of families.

There is also a move to set up nursery schools for the youngest Gypsy children. There is a thriving one at Redbridge, Essex, financed by the film star Yul Brynner.

Lack of education has many disadvantages for the *Rom*. For instance when many Gypsies changed from horse-drawn wagons to trailers, in many cases only ten or so years ago, they were unable to read or write and therefore unable to get driving licences. Even today these men are being prosecuted for driving without the licence they are unable to get simply because they cannot read the Highway Code or fill in the necessary forms.

Not all the changes in today's ever-changing world are

against the interests of the *Rom*. They are forever finding new occupations to replace the old out-of-date ones. There are still plenty of jobs that a self-employed man can do out of doors and with little capital outlay. 'Tarmac-ing' is becoming very popular: with a minimum of equipment a Romany man can re-lay a garden path or a garage drive with tarmac. He can also repair a roof, or trim or cut down trees;

and there are an increasing number to be seen in street markets selling second-hand or 'antique' furniture. There is still plenty of work for a scrap-dealer, although premises for storing the scrap are difficult to come by, and unfortunately most of the official camping-sites don't have what they call a work area in which to keep the scrap.

Perhaps the best change in recent times is the fact that it is no longer necessary, since our entry into the Common Market, to have a work permit for European countries. Romanies are now free to travel between Britain and the Continent, and this opens up many more exciting prospects for Gypsies everywhere, especially as there are plans afoot for establishing official camping-sites in many Western European countries. But with the single exception of Holland, other countries have been even slower than Britain in actually establishing these sites, though prospects for future generations of Romanies seem brighter thanks to the dedicated work of small organizations of persevering Romanies and caring *gorgios*.

Finally, although in some parts of the world Romanies are being forced, at least temporarily, to integrate with the *gorgios*, it is a great mistake to think of the Romanies as a dying race. With their never ceasing vitality and ingenuity they are overcoming the difficulties of living in this modern world, and keeping their independence intact. There is in fact an increase in the Romany population in Britain of about one thousand every year, and the world population is expected to reach ten million by 1980.

Here today and there tomorrow

By day I saw his van in the lane,
Where the moorland rises high,
His little brood watched his ponies move,
As they cropped the grass close by.
Whilst he went hunting, heron-like,
Upstream, from bend to mere,
Sending his mongrel through the sedge
And his whistle carrying clear.

At night I saw his van in the copse
That out of the village lies;
His fire was on the dewy ground,
His hearth beneath bare skies.
And he amongst his chattering brood
Like a gentle chieftain stood;
His fingers danced on his fiddle strings,
His laughter filled the wood.

And who tonight can say where he is?
He has left behind on the green
Two blackened stones and some bluish dust
And a smell of smoke where he's been.
He is not tied to a house in a street,
And his life is sweet as may be.
He can please himself where he goes to roam
And die where God may decree.

Eifion Wyn

Translated from 'Y Sipsiwn' (Caniadau'r Allt, 1927) by J. Glyn Davies.

Taken from 'The Wind on the Heath' by John Sampson published by Chatto & Windus, Pelham Library, London, 1941.

Bibliography

Dialect of the English Gypsies by Smart & Crofton. Asher & Co (1875)

English Gipsies & Their Language by C. Leland. Trübner & Co (1873)

The Gipsies by Jan Yoors. Allen & Unwin

Born on the Straw by Dorothy Strange. Hutchinson.

The Gypsies by Jean-Paul Clebert. Penguin.

A Mysterious People by Charles Duff. Hamish Hamilton.

The Book of Boswell by Silvester Gordon Boswell. Gollancz.

The Romany Way to Health by Charles Bowness. Thorsons Publishers Ltd.

The Roots of Health by Leon Petulengro. Souvenir Press, Pan Books Ltd.

Secrets of Romany Astrology & Palmistry by Leon Petulengro. Souvenir Press; Pan Books Ltd.

If you have enjoyed this PICCOLO Book, you may like to choose your next book from the titles listed on the following pages.

Piccolo Information Books

Geoffrey G. Watson
THE NATURALIST'S HANDBOOK
(illus)   25p

A really useful book for anyone interested in Natural History, packed with information about fossils, rocks, birds, plants and animals and how to find them. Invaluable for fieldwork.

Enid Blyton
BIRDS OF OUR GARDENS (illus)   20p

Enid Blyton tells us how to identify all the common birds and their habits by watching and listening. She also gives lots of information about making bird-tables and feeding.

Jean Stroud
PICCOLO ENCYCLOPEDIA OF
USEFUL FACTS (illus)   30p

A fascinating book with literally thousands of facts on all subjects ranging from the Solar System and Wonders of Nature to Religion and the Arts.

Other Piccolo Books

True Animal Stories

Ken Jones
ORPHANS OF THE SEA (illus)   25p

She was a creamy white furry bundle, 3 feet
long, only a day or two old ... the first of
several hundred orphan seals and other animals
to find refuge with Ken Jones and his family.
This enchanting book – illustrated with lots
of photographs – tells the true story of the
Cornish Seal Sanctuary.

Ernest Dudley
RUFUS: THE STORY OF A FOX   25p

Rufus, born in the wild Scottish Highlands
was just six months old when he came into the
possession of Don MacCaskill, a local forester.
This is the unique true story of a wild creature
accepting captivity.

Eric Delderfield
TRUE ANIMAL STORIES (illus)   25p

**THE SECOND BOOK OF TRUE
   ANIMAL STORIES**   25p

The world of animals is full of surprises and
here are two fascinating books with absorbing
stories about every kind of animal and about
safari parks and lion reserves. For instance,
read about the deep friendship between a
hen and a cat! and many other funny, sad,
puzzling, and amazing stories.